OUT OF THE BOX
THINKING ON
INDIGENOUS
LEADERSHIP

Simple strategies to Create an Empowering Future

For Kirk,
I have heard about
your powerful work & of the
difference you are making
in your community & consequently
in our World.
In gratitude & love,
Vicki & Wendy
♡

GLOBAL
PUBLISHING
G R O U P

Global Publishing Group
Australia • New Zealand • Singapore • America • London

OUT OF THE BOX
THINKING ON
INDIGENOUS
LEADERSHIP

Simple strategies to Create an Empowering Future

Wendy Watego And Vicki Scott

First Edition 2014

National Library of Australia Cataloguing-in-Publication entry

Watego, Wendy, author.
Out of the box thinking on Indigenous leadership : simple
strategies to create an empowering
future / Wendy Watago and Vicki Scott.
ISBN: 9781922118349 (paperback)

    Aboriginal Australians.
    Leadership.
    Community leadership--Australia.
    Civic leaders--Australia.
    Social reformers--Australia.
    Social change--Australia.

Other Authors/Contributors:
Scott, Vicki, author.

362.849915

Published by Global Publishing Group
PO Box 517 Mt Evelyn, Victoria 3796 Australia
Email info@TheGlobalPublishingGroup.com
For Further information about orders:
Phone: +61 3 9739 4686 or Fax +61 3 8648 6871

DEDICATION

We acknowledge our Ancestral Spirits and Elders, past, present and future, and we dedicate this book to all the Aboriginal and Torres Strait Islander people who, since colonisation, have fought for and continue to stand up for the right to retain their land, languages, culture and identity. Their resolve is significant for all of us.

We thank all those who have supported and continue to support Aboriginal and Torres Strait Islander peoples in their journey to self-determination.

The sacredness of 40,000 years of the cultural heritage of our First Australians needs to be recognised in all ways, including in the Australian Constitution.

We acknowledge the whole community who own our shared histories and who share the vision for true reconciliation.

We stand on the shoulders of giants. Thank you for holding the space.

Wendy and Vicki

ACKNOWLEDGEMENTS

There are many people we would like to acknowledge, especially our families – Ken, Lawson and Archie, and Richard, Don and Tara, Beck, Behrouz and Brax – for their longstanding support of us, what we have done over the last 6 years and our vision for a different future. And above all, for their understanding when we have been so preoccupied!

Wendy's parents, Aunty Judy and Uncle Richard Watego, who have supported us personally as well as being a constant part of the STARS Leadership Team. Other members of the STARS Leadership Team including Dr Jackie Huggins AM, for the unconditional support she has shown us over many years and for writing the Foreword; Suzanne Thompson, an amazing woman who shares her gifts of Women's Lore, Healing, Cultural Facilitator and Educator; Sandra Georgiou, the genius behind the *Black Bold and Beautiful* event; as well as Beck who also contributed her unique skills to the final manuscript of the book. You can read more about the Leadership Team at www.StarsLeadershipInstitute.com

Without Ken's Mum Louisa, and Wendy's extended family to hold the fort at home, Wendy could not have been at the frontline so often.

There are a number of mentors and role models who have inspired and encouraged us, including Dr Lowitja O'Donoghue AC CBE, who has also supported us and the work we do over many years; the Honourable Linda Burney MP, Patrick Dodson, Mick Dodson, Ray Martin, Neil Westbury, Evelyn Scott, Alf Lacey, Rachel Atkinson, Noel Pearson, Noela Gorey, Bill Pritchard, Trisch Muller, Jeremy Donovan and Jane Kemp.

We also thank McCullough Robertson Lawyers and Great Big Events who have supported us from the beginning as well as Joel and Heidi Roberts for helping us be more clear in our key messages.

Thank you to Global Publishing Group for their assistance and patience with us!

Last, but far from least, we would also like to thank all the graduates who have attended STARS programs since we began this journey. It has been their feedback and sharing which has encouraged us to continue to develop the programs and to produce this book.

We salute you all in love and gratitude!

BONUS OFFERS

To watch a quick and funny video on how your brain gets wired and your neural networks get developed, go to our website **www.StarsLeadershipInstitute.com** then click on our YouTube channel and watch the video, "*Cheese Cake, Carrot Cake Wired, But Not For Life*".

Keep up to date on the latest news and simple strategies for running your own brain and mastering your emotions. Go to our website **www.StarsLeadershipInstitute.com** and click on "*Resources*," then click on "*My Brain*" you will have instant access to a variety of PDFs you can download immediately.

Go to our book website **www.OutOfTheBoxThinkingIndigenousLeadership.com** and click on "*Free Book Bonuses*," you can subscribe to the *Out of the Box Thinking "thoughts of the week"*. Every week you will receive a profound lesson that will enliven your spirit, touch your heart, empower your life and grow your leadership muscles.

Go to our book website **www.OutOfTheBoxThinkingIndigenousLeadership.com** and click on "*Free Work Booklet*," you can IMMEDIATELY download the work booklet *My Vision: My Success Plan* and begin using it.

If you would like a copy of our one page *My Vision. My Leadership Plan workflow* go to our book website **www.OutOfTheBoxThinkingIndigenousLeadership.com** and click on "*My Vision. My Leadership Plan workflow*" to IMMEDIATELY download a copy.

CONTENTS

FOREWORD BY
DR JACKIE HUGGINS AM

Take your seats and get ready, for this is no ordinary book on Leadership. It is, as they say, definitely "Out of the Box." Having facilitated numerous Leadership workshops all over Australia I can honestly declare that I have not seen anything like it.

Wendy Watego and Vicki Scott educate, train and coach people in a very unique way. There is something very special about the way they operate. I attended one of their programs – a Dada Gana National Indigenous Women's Leadership program held over a 4 month period – and if I had not been there I would not have believed it was possible. This book is based on their core curriculum and it will inspire, impact and transform lives.

Before my eyes I saw women transformed beyond belief. Women who had come from difficult and sad backgrounds, women who were successful in life and their careers, women who were widely travelled and those who had not yet left our shores, women with the smarts and not so smarts, fabulous and outstanding, yet all were seeking something better in their world and ways to go about achieving their dreams.

When you are in the presence of great women it makes you step up a notch yourself. I continually found that I also wanted to be in that space. No matter how experienced, educated or well versed in the universe we are, there is always something to learn. The passion of learning never leaves us and the chapters in this book remind us of how much there is still to learn.

It is done with humility and compassion as it exudes love and wisdom. Every word commands deep thought and reflection. Respect and admiration abounds in each verse. It is meticulous in its true attempts to bring people together and the method of two women from different cultures working so lovingly is a joy to witness.

Leadership now requires us to be thinking and doing things in different ways. The world is changing so fast and if we don't keep up and continue to develop ourselves as leaders we will struggle. Leadership is an inside job just as much as it is an outside job and as you read this book you will begin to tap into your own strengths, truths and capacities. Remaining strong in our culture and identity is vital to the integrity of our success as a leader. This book teaches you that.

However, do not think this is a "soft-sell" because it isn't. The lessons of life never are. No matter how fine our lives have been there have been tragedies along the way and no one escapes that. The book shows us how to overcome these and get on with what is planned for us.

Both Wendy and Vicki are highly experienced leaders and they live what they teach. They bring a whole new life to the world of leadership that you didn't know existed within you. They have worked with Indigenous and non-Indigenous people all across Australia. Their techniques are attuned to those who are open to explore the crevices of their mind that sometimes lie dormant until they are awakened. This then feeds into participants' Leadership ideals and possibilities, reinforcing their individual strengths and weaknesses which they in turn acknowledge and work on.

This is a "must have" book for anyone working in Leadership and improving the outcomes for the human race. I have been privileged to have played a small role and to have been a part of this magnificent journey.

INTRODUCTION

"We are our own salvation...Our destiny is in our own hands...we cannot leave it to churches, government, international pressures, dreams or the goodwill of others.

Charles Perkins

CHAPTER 1

Have You Ever Received A Message From Your Heart?

Yurra, Yurra. Welcome, welcome to our book, *"Out Of The Box Thinking On Indigenous Leadership. Simple Strategies To Create An Empowering Future."*

My name is Wendy and I am Quandamooka Goori and together with Vicki we would firstly like to acknowledge and pay our deepest respect to the spiritual ancestors and elders whose Lands this book will pass through. We respect the sacredness of your sovereignty and continued connections with your culture and your country, and even though our landscapes may be different, we share with you a strength and pride in who we are as First Nations peoples, and a history that sometimes makes us cry, but most times makes us proud.

We thank you for the battles your Mob have fought, and continue to fight, for the rights to and the protection of our mother our land, our people, our dreaming and our culture. We are sorry for the many good lives that were lost and we remember with honour the sacrifices that were made at the face of invasion, colonisation and the history which has continued to follow.

We thank you for reading this book and as it moves through your sacred land, please know that it comes from our hearts and we hope that it touches yours. This book originates from the work Vicki and I have been doing for the last six years in the areas of healing and leadership. **It signifies our commitment to making a difference in the daily lives of First Nations peoples and those who are our families, friends, communities, work colleagues, supporters and advocates.**

It is with respect, honour, integrity and love that we have written *"Out Of The Box Thinking on Indigenous Leadership"* and it is our intention that the book will bring tremendous value to the lives of ALL who read it.

We will share with you some more about ourselves soon but right now here is a little sneak peak at what the book is about and why we have written it.

"Warning! This Book Is Not Your Ordinary Book On Leadership."

You are holding in your hands a living resource. Let's be clear right from the start that it is not an ordinary book about Blackfulla leadership.

It is written specifically for Blackfullas who:

- Are already leaders within their homes, communities, organisations and departments.
- Are aspiring to be leaders and take up leadership roles.
- Want to expand their life and grow their leadership.

And Whitefellas who:

- Currently work in leadership positions within First Nations organisations, programs and departments.
- Are working with First Nations organisations, programs and departments.

Six years ago Vicki and I co-founded an organisation called STARS Institute of Learning and Leadership and for the last four years we have focussed our energies on working specifically with First Nations people from across the country who have been in senior management and leadership positions within their communities, departments, organisations and the private sector.

What we have found is that although the participants who have worked with us are usually well educated, have a wealth of life experience, have participated in other leadership programs, have work expertise, are often anchored in their culture and are proud of their identity as First Nations people, they are suffering in some way from the insidious and silent impacts of unresolved inter-generational trauma. And they don't even know it – OR how it is stopping them from reaching their full potential.

As Dr Jackie Huggins, who was a member of our leadership team during a 6 month national leadership program said, *"STARS programs empower people to begin healing from inter-generational trauma. They come away with a greater purpose and power in their life and leadership than they have ever experienced before."*

We do not mould a specific type of leader. We allow for individuals to define their own leadership and their own strength which filters back to their community. It is not about ticking boxes or completing modules but strengthening their capacity to be powerful in all situations. The standard of excellence is set at the beginning so that becomes the "norm" – not a *"close enough is good enough/that will do"* attitude.

We know that **until the inner transformation matches the outer opportunities**, it is unlikely that the full benefit of the dollars being spent will achieve the desired outcome that is sustainable over time.

Why the book? *Out of the Box Thinking on Indigenous Leadership* **IS** our programs in a book. It is what our graduates and our advocates have asked for.

Here's what they have said:

"We want to take the program home with us and share it with other people in our lives…"

"We as leaders are just as hurt and wounded as the people we are serving."

"Everyone has to do this work…"

"This program gives people strategies for dealing with lateral violence..."

"This work needs to be taught in schools…"

In a nutshell this book is intended to:

1. Expose a silent national lie that has travelled throughout history and constrained all Australians but has had the most devastating impact on First Nations peoples.

2. Empower you to break free from the shackles of the past.

3. Strengthen your identity muscles and usher in a new era of Blackfulla leadership.

4. Hand you back the power to transform your life and grow into your vision for leadership.

Pretty Bold Intentions, Hey?

The challenges us Blackfullas are facing today are signs that change is imminent. But what if part of that change means we have to be prepared to start thinking in new ways? Life is moving so darn fast that we can no longer continue to think, believe and do things in the same old ways and expect that results are going to improve and that transformations will naturally follow.

The same issues we are standing for today are the same old issues our grandparents and aunties and uncles and families were fighting for back in 1972 with the establishment of the Aboriginal Tent Embassy. It's a recycling of the same issues throughout history. True or true?

A paradigm shift is required quickly if there is to be a new future for our children that does not look like the past or replicate the present. It's so awesome to see that on a national and state level there are lots of good things happening out there that are getting real life-altering results that are beginning to shift the future paradigm of what it means to be a proper deadly Blackfulla in the 21st century. Things like the Stronger Smarter Institute based in Queensland, the National Centre of Indigenous Excellence located in Sydney and the inspirational work of National Indigenous Television NITV, just to name a few.

The question is, what can we do to begin this paradigm shift? **Out of the Box thinking on Indigenous Leadership** recognises that we are all leaders within our own lives and that we all have an inner vision for who we are and what we want, for our families and for our communities. This book is intended to empower you with the tools and the mindset which could potentially change your life forever.

Sounds fishy doesn't it? We can hear you screaming criticism at us from here and if we were you, we'd probably be doubtful too. We promise you that some of what you read in this book will blow your mind and, when you learn about the sickness of the silent national lie, some of it will make you wild.

Look people, to be honest, **Out of the Box Thinking on Indigenous Leadership** is not a leadership book for everybody. It is designed to have you look at your life and your leadership through a new set of eyes.

Here is the thing. You will never be able to perform well under pressure or sustain the most successful of results and feel truly fulfilled if you are still carrying around your baggage and other people's baggage from your past. Your spirit knows this to be true!

> Never doubt that a small group of thoughtful, committed citizens can change the world; indeed, it's the only thing that ever has.
>
> **Margaret Mead**

So here is an important question you need to ask yourself before reading any further; *"Is this* book *really for me?"*

Have we scared you off yet? We promise you it will be a cracker of a read, as you will experience a swirl of emotions and new and inspiring ideas. It is not just a book, it is an ultimate experience. This book is for those of you who are genuinely ready and committed to move your life and your leadership into a whole new realm of awesome-ness.

If you:

1. Think this book is the magic pill and expect after reading it that everything will fall into place with little or no committed action from you, then please give the book to someone who is willing to take action.

2. Are skeptical and doubtful that the teachings offered in this book will work for you, then please give the book to someone who is open and optimistic.

3. Think you will whine and moan the whole time you are reading it, and maybe not even finish reading it, then please give the book to someone who is more willing to be inspired and excited about the new possibilities for their life and their future.

You are probably wondering by now, how does **Out of the Box Thinking on Indigenous Leadership** work its magic and what benefits will I get from using it?

Good questions. Enjoy the book!

> If you want to awaken all of humanity, then awaken all of yourself.
>
> If you want to eliminate the suffering in the world, then eliminate all that is dark and negative in yourself.
>
> Truly, the greatest gift that you have to give is that of your own self transformation.
>
> **Lao Tsu**

WENDY'S STORY

I was born Wendy Watego and on my mother's side of the family I am a Goenpil, Nughie, Noonuccal Goori (Aboriginal) from Minjerribah – North Stradbroke Island – which is part of the Quandamooka Nation.

My Mother is Judy Watego, she was born to Archie and Edna Newfong. My Pop, Uncle Archie as he was fondly known, was an Aborigine. His Mum was a traditional woman from Clermont who was moved off her Country and brought to the Myora Mission on Stradbroke Island. Pop's Dad was from Rotuma Island in Fiji and he and four other men sailed to Stradbroke in a canoe.

My Nanny Edna came from the Crouch and Campbell families. The Campbell family were pioneers in the fishing and boating industry in Moreton Bay or what is traditionally known as Quandamooka. Nana was a great sportswoman and played women's cricket. She was a left arm spin bowler. In 1934 Nan was selected to represent Queensland and play against the touring English women's team. In more recent times she was inducted into the Aboriginal and Torres Strait Islander Sports Hall of Fame.

Mum's brother, Uncle John Newfong, was a deadly Blackfulla media pioneer. He was the first Indigenous journalist to be employed as a journalist in the mainstream print media and he wrote for papers such as The Australian and The Sydney Morning Herald. Uncle John was a dedicated activist and instrumental in the Aboriginal movement of the 60s and 70s which included being the chief spokesperson for the Aboriginal Tent Embassy in Canberra in 1972. In 2008, the John Newfong Media Award was launched by the Centre for Aboriginal Independence and Enterprise to acknowledge Uncle John's contribution to journalism. It is awarded annually to recognise the great work of

First Nations journalists. A street in Canberra called Newfong has been named after him in recognition of his contributions.

On my Father's side of the family, we are South Sea Islanders from Mare Island in New Caledonia. Dad's ancestors were brought to Australia as "kanakas." They were sugar slaves, brought over here to work on the sugar plantations in far north Queensland. Dad's Mob also have Aboriginal ancestry which we have been actively tracing and have found some connections with the Bundjalung Mob in New South Wales.

Dad is the second eldest and comes from a big family of 12 brothers and sisters. Their family home was in Mt Gravatt, Queensland. Dad's parents died when he was only 19. What was remarkable about Dad and his family was that in spite of departmental pressure, after Nana and Grandad Watego died, to split the family up, Dad and his older brothers and sisters managed to keep all 12 of their young family together. This was very unusual, especially for Black families during this time and a great achievement.

I have two Sisters, Angela and Nicole, and two Brothers, Anthony and Michael, who you will hear about throughout the book. I had a younger brother, Lloyd, who passed away due to a heart condition, at just six weeks old.

I am married to my highschool sweetheart, Ken Ittensohn, and we have two beautiful energetic sons, Lawson Ike Mirrigimpi who is now 13 and Archie Erich Bummeira who is now 4. Ken's Dad, Erich, is Swiss and his Mum, Louisa, is Dutch. They were both immigrants.

I've come from the education and schooling profession which you will also hear more about throughout the book. After participating in an Anthony Robbins program fifteen years ago I made a decision to leave teaching and move into coaching.

I've worked in the area of healing and leadership for 13 years now. When I met Vicki Scott I knew this woman was very special; she's got a good heart. What was really interesting was that Vicki and I come from very different places, from very different cultures, a different generation and have had very different life experiences but we have a profound connection. And the connection includes a shared vision to make a difference in the daily lives of individuals and communities.

This book will be written in the main part as me speaking to you, which is how we lead our leadership clinics and other programs. Vicki and I are clear about where each of our individual gifts and talents lie and we work to those strengths. In Chapter 9, *Your Vision Your Victory*, Vicki will share her experience as project director for *Corroboree* 2000, including the unforgettable Walk for Reconciliation across the Sydney Harbour Bridge.

VICKI'S STORY

Firstly, I would like to acknowledge the traditional owners of our country, Australia, and our Elders, past and present, for holding the space for *what else is possible*? I would also like to acknowledge each individual Aboriginal person as a descendant of the oldest surviving culture in the world, and each Torres Strait Islander person as a descendant of Australia's other First Nations people, whose history also dates back thousands of years.

I was born Vicki Urquhart in Barcaldine in Central Western Queensland, the traditional country of the Iningai people. I am the eldest daughter in a family of seven children. I saw my mother suffer with depression and in later life with episodes of psychosis (out of touch with reality) and paranoia. She was a remarkable woman.

Mum worked initially as a 'domestic' on sheep properties and was encouraged by an astute employer to pursue the more challenging and rewarding career of nursing. She trained as a nurse in Brisbane where she served throughout World War II. Following the death of a soldier brother in New Guinea in 1945, Mum went to Barcaldine to help her mother and continue her nursing. There, she met my father while nursing his grandmother and later married him.

Sixty-plus years later, her seven children can still gather in harmony and have meaningful conversations. She did an exceptional job, especially considering her limited early educational and social opportunities. Despite her personal and parental achievements, she lacked self-belief and self-confidence. There was no self-acceptance.

Her burning desire to fit the mould of the ideal wife and mother in a small country town in the 1950s meant she endured postnatal depression in silence.

When I realised I also suffered powerlessness, due to postnatal depression after my first baby, I thought, *"There has to be another way: we need to learn some different skills that serve us as human beings."*

I began work at 14 years of age. By the age of 18, I was personal assistant to the Governor-General and later worked in the Prime Minister's Department and the Queensland Premier's Department – two major 'centres of power' in Australia. I also worked for Lowitja O'Donoghue when she was the Chairperson of the Aboriginal and Torres Strait Islander Commission, a seminal period for Indigenous rights and recognition that included the Senate debate on the *Native Title Act 1993*.

I was privileged to travel with Lowitja through the Anangu Pitjantjatjara Yankunytjatjara (APY) Lands. Lowitja is a Yankunytjatjara woman, so I was in her Country, and this was a profound learning experience for me – to glimpse the meaning of country through an Elder's eyes.

Who has the power to make real progress?

Corroboree 2000, for which I was project director, culminated in 250,000 Australians walking together across Sydney Harbour Bridge in acknowledgement of Indigenous rights and recognition. The event was even reported in the *New York Times*. While it was a spectacular and unequivocal display of solidarity with Indigenous Australians, I was left wondering if it had made, or could make, a lasting difference.

Similarly, I wondered about the legacy of a gathering as powerful as the Commonwealth Heads of Government Meeting 2002, of which I was the director for the Queensland Government. It was attended by the Queen and 53 presidents and prime ministers. When it concluded, I felt it had done nothing to alleviate the suffering of the people of Zimbabwe under the megalomaniac, Robert Mugabe.

The key question I needed an answer to was: "**WHERE is the power** to make a difference in the daily lives of people?"

About ten years ago, I became more aware of how devastating it could be on the health and wellbeing of an individual to feel powerless. I was diagnosed with an auto-immune disease, and this was closely followed by our daughter, then 24, having a tumour that no-one had seen before and about which could not give us any clear hope. Thankfully, our daughter had a good result.

I, on the other hand, struggled and had a breakdown. Whilst this was an extremely testing time it was also an important time of growth and renewal; a time of inner healing. Now my resilience muscles have strengthened and I respect the importance of the power of healing for the good functioning of the body, mind and spirit.

Many times over the years, I have gone off track but what always brought me back was being able to have my eye on what was important to me, really knowing why it was important and being very clear about the impact on me and others if I did not achieve my vision.

To this day, a key question I ask myself is, "*Is this working for me?*".... You know the truth when you hear it. ☺

Why a White Woman?

For a long time I struggled with what I was doing in the area of Indigenous Leadership. However, I believe this is not a Blackfella issue, it belongs to all of us. This country was colonised on the basis of the lie that, "*Blackfellas aren't as good as Whitefellas.*"

This lie needs to be voiced out loud, you cannot heal what you do not acknowledge. Human potential cannot be realised without healing from the inside out. It is an inside job! There is much healing that needs to happen for our First Nations people and us Whitefellas too.

To the wider community, I say we cannot continue to bandaid over this issue. I acknowledge inter-generational trauma is real for most human beings but, here in Australia, one key factor is a result of the ongoing impact of the colonisation process which impacts on both Black and White Australians. And we – all of us here at this time – have the power to do something about it.

The statistics tell us there has been some progress, but despite all the goodwill and the current focus on programs and actions, something is still missing, something is still not working. Right now, many of us don't even believe we HAVE a choice, we cannot see that we have power.

Whilst unresolved trauma continues to be passed down from one generation to the next, the foundations for change will remain weak. Until the inner transformation matches the outer opportunities, it does not matter how much money we throw into what are great programs, no long-term sustainable change can happen.

> You don't build a house on insecure foundations. As any builder knows, the footings influence the structural soundness of an entire building.
>
> **Jason Glanville,** *CEO of the National Centre of Indigenous Excellence*

It has been my privilege to have founded the STARS Institute of Learning and Leadership with Wendy Watego. We share the same vision of empowering people to have real "self" determination.

This is not a "do as I say" book. The knowledge and tools we share are what Wendy and I use in our own daily lives, they are what we share with our own families and what we train leaders and professionals in.

For me and Wendy there is no separation between work and home, or black and white. As Sidney Poitier said, in talking about his role in "A Raisin in the Sun"…"*the power of the piece was in its basic human emotions.... the play was a lesson in what humans are really, really all about. People aren't about being black or white. Black and white in the face of real issues are mere cosmetics.*"

I wish you well in YOUR personal journey of life and contribution to a greater good, and remember..... we don't have to do it all on our own ☺

SECTION ONE

"

Our life pattern was created by the
government policies and are forever
with me, as though an invisible
anchor around my neck.

Confidential submission 338, Victoria.
Bringing them Home Report 1997.

"

CHAPTER 2

They Laughed When We Said We're Exposing The National Lie

Our intention in Section One is to bring your consciousness to a Silent National Lie (SNL) that has infected our psyche and stone-walled our leadership capacity as Blackfullas. This SNL has its origin based in racism, oppression, genocide and exclusion, and over time its injustice has become institutionalised and unrecognisable.

There are many national colonial lies that are now rightfully being exposed and this one, like the others, is toxic. It breaches human rights and is off the radar of consciousness for many Australians, yet it is embedded within our emotional and spiritual landscape, continuing to silently shape and shift the identity of our nation.

This SNL sailed in on the ships with the colonisers, it is responsible for causing the exclusion of First Nations peoples in the drafting of the Australian Constitution and it played an instrumental role in the inclusion of special laws which legalised racial discrimination within the Constitution pertaining to controlling the lives of Aborigines and Torres Strait Islanders. The SNL was also a key inspiration for the White Australia Policy which was one of the first Acts of Parliament after Federation in 1901.

We thought and hoped that the 1967 Referendum would have put an end to the SNL but it did not; instead it pushed the lie underground. In more recent times, we thought and hoped that perhaps the Federal Government's apology to the Stolen Generation in February 2008 would have begun a nationwide conversation and a process of real healing and true reconciliation. But it did not.

Instead, the historical baggage of the SNL ramped up the urgency of the Northern Territory Intervention known now as the *Stronger Futures Legislation* and over-shadowed all the good that potentially could have come from the Apology.

Perhaps the future Referendum to recognise Aborigines and Torres Strait Islanders in the Constitution and remove discrimination from it, will bring the SNL to the end of its era?

Only time will tell.

This section of the book is not intended to be full of sad stories or pointing fingers and blaming others for the existence of the SNL. It is also not intended to collude with a victimhood status that is considered by some Australians to be part of our identity as Aborigines and Torres Strait Islanders.

It is intended to expose the SNL and to begin some new, constructive, healthy conversation about how the SNL originated and has manifested throughout history and how it is still impacting all Australians today, particularly First Nations peoples. It plays havoc with our lives and our leadership.

The section also offers practical ideas about things we can begin doing ourselves to bring an end to it.

One of the many things that personally excited me about exposing the SNL is a deep appreciation and inner spiritual knowing that in spite of the grave history that has preceded us, and continues to challenge us because of the lie, we as First Nations peoples have always been victorious. We are still here and growing stronger, doing all we can in our areas of expertise to liberate ourselves, our peoples and inevitably Australia from the chains of a stained past.

My 'Old people' continue to teach me the sacredness of my birthright as a Goenpil, Nughie, Noonuccal, Quandamooka Goori and South Sea Islander. I know without a doubt that my Blackfulla culture and identity has never been truly lost and can never be taken from me.

The Dreaming of my people is safely encoded within my DNA, just as much as it is ever-present in every facet of the Land. As I continue to learn from the sacred text of Mother Earth and my Elders, my identity deepens and calls forth the responsibilities I have to Country and to humanity. Knowing who I am, where I come from, who my Mob are and why and how I am to contribute, is my greatest and strongest asset as a Blackfulla leader in the 21st century.

In exposing this SNL we wanted to give you a new lens to look through and contemplate from. It's important to not only know about how this SNL is woven throughout our history but also to take time to reflect upon it, talk about it, gain a genuine understanding of why and how this SNL is at the foundation of all the challenges we face in life today.

We recommend that you begin conversations about it with both Blackfullas and Whitefellas to see if it does exist in your world. In fact, it may not be your experience at all. The significance in having conversations is that you will quickly distinguish the SNL as it comes in a language all of its own – usually the language of deficit.

The value of talking about the SNL is that we declare responsibility for empowering ourselves. Conversations such as these are now, more than ever before, a vital tool in giving us access to unlocking areas of our lives where we know we have been 'blocked up' and where inner healing needs to happen. Only then, can we truly work effectively to empower our families, our communities, our workplaces and others towards self-determination.

As leaders who are here to assert change and lead in transformation, it is our duty to work on ourselves as well. In doing so, it honours our ancestry and positively acknowledges those trailblazers, activists and leaders who, in spite of this SNL, have championed before us and helped prepare the ground for new leaders to emerge and contribute.

Let us not wait for our existing leaders to step down or hand the baton on to us, they all have a huge enough job to do, let us step up to the plate – the time is NOW!

Just as importantly, if we modern Blackfullas become sufferers of historical amnesia, we are blind and helpless to see how we are entrapped within the SNL and numb to its impacts on our lives and our leadership.

The Silent National Lie Exposed...

We have read many history books, including those written by First Nations people from Australia and other colonised countries, on how colonisation has had a similar impact on Indigenous people around the world. But in the work we have done nationally in the last four years with Aboriginal and Torres Strait Islander leaders and professionals, and Whitefella leaders who work with us Fullas, we have evidenced that the silent ugly 21st century national lie still exists.

"Blackfullas aren't as good as Whitefellas"

There it is! The lie is plain – and not so simple – but it is out of the box. "Blackfullas aren't as good as Whitefellas." Sucks hey...?

We unapologetically won't water it down in order to make you feel comfortable because that is what hoodwinks our attention, disguises the lie's insidiousness and has pushed it underground for so long.

The survivors and families of the victims of the September 11 terrorist attack on the USA are not expected to water down the aftermath of their pain and injustices, neither are the Jewish people of the Holocaust nor our very own ANZAC Diggers.

As you will discover, the SNL has been called many different things in its lifetime which has led to its pervasive nature. In current times, if people are aware of the SNL they are too scared to talk about it openly because they are afraid of being called a racist if they're White and, if they're a Blackfulla, either a self-pitying victim, or being perceived as booting the victim. The history of the SNL, like so much of Blackfulla history, has been buried for so very long.

Although the truth of Blackfulla history was not written into the Whitefella history books, it was written into the hearts and spirits of all us Blackfullas. Many of our traditional sacred stories and Creation stories have now been replaced with sorry stories of trauma and tragedy.

Sorry stories which have been borne as a result of the SNL and have been passed down through the generations.

> Consider that our children are now building their identity as a Blackfulla based on these sorry stories of inter-generational trauma, racism and discrimination. If this SNL remains secret, then our children and our grandchildren become the future custodians of the SNL.

The colonising process did not stop in 1967 when we were finally counted in the Australian Census, 179 years after Australia was colonised. Colonisation, particularly assimilation, is an ongoing, well established, elusive practice that has the ability to shape change over time. It attempts to hide behind the veils of mainstreaming and 'racial progress.' But statistics (2014 Closing the Gap Report) in education, health, employment, housing, home ownership and life expectancy are revealing that in spite of perceived 'racial progress' and moves towards mainstreaming, something is still not working.

Whilst we acknowledge that there is a high level of goodwill present in so many sections of Australian society, there still exists a collective unconsciousness of denial around the existence and acceptance of the SNL and the significance it has on determining the history of Australia.

You only have to watch, read or listen to the daily news, follow social media or listen to your mates or colleagues when racial issues arise in the news to hear how racially fatigued Australians are becoming. This is across the board: with boat people, the war on terrorism, telemarketers with Indian accents, Japanese tourists not swimming between the flags and women wearing burkas, to mention a few incidents. Eruptions of racially-motivated violence are on the increase on public transport and, whilst witnesses agonise over it, they are reluctant to step in for fear of their own safety.

Google search '*white supremacy in Australia*' and see just how alive and thriving racism and the SNL is.

Or, if you really want to challenge yourself, fly the Aboriginal or Torres Strait Islander flag outside your house for 12 months and see what reactions you attract.

The sad irony is that whilst Australians continue to complain and whinge about racial differences they still stand by the Aussie ethos that we live in the Lucky Country – '*the Land of a Fair Go* for all!*'

True Blue Aussies suffer from the Fair Go Syndrome…

Interestingly for First Nations peoples '*the Land of a Fair Go*' ethos applies only to some of us Blackfullas, not all of us. Consider that the '*Fair Go Syndrome*' is a by-product of the SNL and has been effective in feeding our country's addiction to a belief that anyone and everyone can 'make it' regardless of cultural and economic obstacles. It gives the illusion that if some Blackfullas have made it in the White man's world – yes, the acceptable exceptions – then all Blackfullas should be able to get over the past, stop being angry and do the same!

How many times have you felt sick in the guts when someone says to you, *"I'm not racist but if you can do it why can't the rest of them get off their…and make something of their lives?"* Or the other classic comment, *"…but you're different, you're not like the other…!"* I know I have probably offended people when, surprisingly to them, I don't take such comments as a compliment.

The mainstream media has now started to sensationalise and bestow almost a celebrity status on those Blackfullas who are rightfully successful and contribute to the wider community as well as their own, at the same time as continuing to stereotype and exclude those Blackfullas who are not. It is like, if you fail then all Blackfullas fail but if you succeed then you are the exception, you are one of the 'good ones.' This type of media selection and segregation works to define us as the good Blackfullas – the superior Blacks who have moved "from the dog house to the penthouse!"

Then you have the bad Blackfullas – the inferior Blacks who are drunk, violent, unemployed, deviant and dysfunctional, and who of course consciously choose to wallow in poverty, dependency and victimhood.

The media-invoked fear of the SNL denies the reality that all First Nations people grapple with every day, regardless of the prominence others apply to us. This *'Fair Go Syndrome'* presents new challenges for us as first nation leaders as it upholds an undistinguished social Darwinism mentality of survival of the fittest.

As a country we have accepted misinformation fed to us by the media and become emotionally shut down in order to survive this SNL, concealing the realities and consequences it brings with owning up to it and taking responsibility for the perpetuation of it. This enables the lie to remain dormant within us like a social sickness that can't be healed because it can't be talked about openly and honestly.

Racism is Like An Aussie-ism…

Nowadays it is not uncommon for a Whitefella to have never even said hello or had a conversation with a First Nations person. Yet due to the effectiveness of mainstream media's imagery and commentary of us Fullas and our affairs, Aussies have been programmed through the mass media to either pity, despise or ignore us, or be frightened or wary of us.

And if we don't fit a stereotypical image then we can't be a real Blackfulla. Whichever way, we continue to be portrayed as not being good enough.

This dehumanises us even further and enables armchair racism to bubble up and the SNL to be washed down with a wine or a stubby after work.

Interestingly, when asked, 77% of people believed Australians are racist and 44% of Australians agreed that they are a casual racist and do not want to change (*Racism in Aboriginal Australia. Creative Spirits website www.CreativeSpirits.info*). There certainly is a very strong element of casual racism in Australia says Gillian Triggs, president of the Australian Human Rights Commission. Between June 2012 and June 2013, racial vilification complaints to the commission increased by 19%.

Perhaps many people don't realise that what they are saying or how they are behaving is racist, either that or they have become better at hiding it – usually behind the veil of Aussie larrikinism, the backyard BBQ, watching the footy or sharing a joke around the water cooler at work. This somehow takes the edge off the SNL and makes it okay to be a little bit racist – depending on the situation of course! According to research done by the Australian Reconciliation Barometer in 2012 only a small minority of both Whitefellas and Blackfullas agreed that "non-indigenous Australians are superior to Indigenous Australians (2012 p. 35)."

We would suggest that over time White Australia has been socially and culturally conditioned not to recognise the institutionalised trickiness and the covert sophistication of the SNL in action. For example, people don't notice the lack of Black faces on mainstream television in programs such as soapies or commercials or even as a television journalist. They do notice that when Blackfullas are on the mainstream TV, it is usually advertising tourism, in a negative news report or in a short term tokenistic or stereotypical role in a soapie.

So there is a challenge when many Aussies do overtly bump up against the SNL such as when someone tells a racist joke like, "*What do you call an Abo that does well on an IQ test? Answer: A cheat.*" (January 2014, a joke told at a New Year's Eve party by a group of non-Indigenous party-goers where a personal Whitefella friend of mine was present and shocked and left the party without addressing the joke). They are not sure how to deal with the SNL or racism in a constructive way. Most times they say nothing just like my friend did. It is easier to ignore it and not make a fuss in order to be accepted and liked by the group.

Belonging is a human need. A sense of belonging is a very strong motivator which buys people's silence and it is something that the SNL relies upon in modern times to keep it in existence.

How Do You Know You Are White?

If you are a White person and walking down the street, you don't think about being White. Your "Whiteness" makes you invisible. You are not noticed by others because you look like them and you blend in. You really don't realise your Whiteness until you go to a Blackfulla event such as a NAIDOC week function and are surrounded by Blackfullas and Blackfulla culture. Then you become aware of your Whiteness as a difference. It's not bad or wrong, it is just different.

It is just the same for you menfolk. You become conscious you're a man when you are surrounded by women. As grownups we are conscious we are adults when we are surrounded by children. Make sense?

Whitefella Walking In Blackfulla Shoes…

Now, imagine for a moment what it is like to be a minority here in the *Land of a Fair Go*? Fair Dinkum Mate. Suppose for a moment what it would be like if Blackfulla culture was the dominant culture. Black faces were what you saw when you turned on your TV, with the occasional White face playing a stereotypical or tokenistic role. Black voices, songs and issues were what you heard when you listened to the radio and in the news any White issues were very rare and usually reported negatively.

Every media campaign, politician and policy direction was targeted towards advancing Indigenous people and down-playing the issues of White people.

Imagine if the richest people and powerbrokers in the Land of Oz were Aborigines and Torres Strait Islanders.

What would your life be like if you were taken away from your mother when you were 3 years old because you have some Blackfulla blood in you and you were put into a dormitory with other kids just like you? You were told your mother didn't want you so forget about her and your Whitefella culture because it is wrong and evil. You were beaten if you cried for your mother, ridiculed if you wet the bed or showed anxiety or stress. In order to cope, you shut down emotionally. When you were a teenager you turned to alcohol to numb your pain and you became a parent at 16. What kind of parent would that make you?

What would you say to Blackfullas when they asked you an offensive question about your Aussie-ality such as, "*Are you a full blooded White Aussie or a half-caste or quarter-caste Australian? If your mother's people are of British convict descent and your Dad's Dutch, and he came here under the White Australia policy, then surely you can't be a real true blue Whitefella!*

Suppose you knew because you were White that for generations your family and your culture have been brutalised and continue to be publicly excluded and branded as being inferior, bad, wrong, shameful, evil, deficient and dysfunctional…?

How do you think that would impact your thinking and identity as a White person? How would it shape your thinking towards the dominant Blackfulla culture? What kind of leader would that make you?

Things that make you go hmmmm…

Blackness Is A Way Of Being...

As First Nations people, most of us are proud of our Blackness. It is a sacred way of being in the world. We live it like a badge of honour, secure in the knowledge that we are part of the longest surviving culture in the world. We are strong in our identity and culture and we have a positive outlook on life and the future, whilst enjoying the benefits and luxuries of modernisations.

But we also live a life with the consciousness that we are Black, even those of us who have fair skin. We live daily, knowing that some people won't immediately like, trust or accept us because we are an Aborigine or Torres Strait Islander.

We are conscious that we are being watched when we go into shops; that women will cross the street or hold more tightly onto their bags if a Black man is coming towards them; people get uncomfortable if there are more than ten of us Fullas picnicking in the park with our families; that people avoid us and silently label us as angry and radical if we are wearing any clothing which depicts our flags or voices our identity; that we are viewed with suspicion and scepticism if we are too highly educated or our skin is too White; that taxi drivers won't stop for us; that landlords won't rent to us; that we are overlooked for jobs and even in spite of our leadership prowess on the sporting field we are still called apes, boongs, cannibals, coons, Abos, niggers and Black bastards.

Do we think that being born Indigenous makes it harder to achieve here in the *Land of a Fair Go*? A big fat super-sized YES according to research responses from both Indigenous and non-Indigenous people from the 2008, 2010 and 2012 Australian Reconciliation Barometer.

This modernised national lie – *"Blackfullas aren't as good as Whitefellas"* – has existed for generations and has almost become normalised for us Blackfullas. We have been, and continue to be, defined by White Australia as the 'Aboriginal problem.'

For us Blackfullas it's like being born with a racism radar attached to our heart and it operates 24/7 in order to keep us safe and out of harm's way. Most of us can smell racism and the stench of the *"Blackfullas aren't as good as Whitefellas"* lie a mile away, even if we can't always articulate it or point it out, we know it's there.

"Racism is a constant background noise in the lives of Aboriginal and Torres Strait Islander people." (Submission by Victorian Aboriginal Child Care Agency National Anti-Racism Strategy 2012).

"More than a quarter of Aboriginal people report that they often experience racism in their everyday lives" (Sheehan 2012 p. 86).

I Got Sucked Into This Lie…

I have experienced the *"Blackfullas aren't as good as Whitefellas"* lie myself and wore it like an invisible shackle around my ankle for much of my professional life as an educator. On the outside I appeared confident and competent, the epiphany of a highly successful and upwardly mobile Black woman. But inside, the thought of *"I'm not good enough because I'm Black"* was right there with me like a silent partner continually messing with my mind.

The constant presence of this SNL impacted how I made decisions, determined how much risk I was willing to take, how I formed relationships, who I formed relationships with, how I managed staff, taught in classrooms and led schools. It had me put myself under constant pressure to become a high achiever, a role model, a results producer.

Because I thought *"I wasn't good enough"* I had to be ten times better than anyone else, including my own Mob.

Talk about emotionally exhausting. I was so culturally disconnected, I stopped listening to my Ancestors, I made poor life choices, I was restless and unhappy – I just didn't know it at the time. For a while I used partying and yarndi to numb my pain. I was a breakdown waiting to happen and indeed, I hit a brick wall big time.

What is most alarming was discovering it wasn't just me that had been brainwashed to buy into this lie. Vicki and I have found in the work we do that many other First Nations leaders, in spite of all their spectacular achievements and their diversity in age and location, have the same or similar 'sorry story.'

Even if we didn't intellectually believe it, at some level our Spirit and our body had internalised this insidious SNL and we either became a victim to it or perpetrators of it.

The more I awakened to the origins of my own issues and battles, which festered from the SNL, and reflected on my own family's suffering because they too were trapped inside it, the more I was able to recognise the same wounds in others.

Part of the wickedness of growing up with the SNL is that we Blackfullas have *grown into* the SNL.

> The root of the challenges we all face collectively as First Nations peoples in the 21st century is not the trauma stories of the past and what has been done to us. Rather, it is what this systemised trauma of brainwashing has caused us to *think* and *feel* about ourselves and what we are capable of.

Consider that collectively, as Aborigines and Torres Strait Islanders, we are living in an unrecognisable perpetual state of 'sorry business.'

While you are reading this book, listen to the whispers of your heart. Consider that you too, at some level, have been infected and impacted by the "*Blackfullas aren't as good as Whitefellas*" lie.

This is why it is so important that, now more than ever before, we begin engaging in *new* conversations about defining who we are as Aborigines and Torres Strait Islanders in this modern world. It is important for us to begin transforming the old imposed paradigms which have chained us to the past. It is important that we are futuristic in our thinking about the legacy we want for our great, great grandkids.

" You Can't Have True Reconciliation
Without The Truth.

(Professor Gracelyn Smallwood
2014) "

CHAPTER 3

How We've Been Brainwashed To Believe We Are Inferior

HISTORICAL ROOTS – "Blackfullas Aren't As Good As Whitefellas!"

How Did The Rumour Get Started?

The modernised lie, "Blackfullas aren't as good as Whitefellas," was born from racism and capitalism. It is intrinsically linked to the black inferiority/white superiority belief which was reflective of the political global landscape of imperialism of the time.

The black inferiority/white superiority myth began in the United States in the 17th century to justify using racial slavery as a legalised means to build and expand the economic growth of the ruling class. Once British and European indentured servants were on the decline, leaders of the colonies feared there would be uprisings among the poor, landless whites (www.slaveryinamerica.org).

The solution to the constant threat of rebellion from the landless poor? Raise the status of the poorest whites in the colony by instituting a system of racial slavery.

Supported by racist 16th century philosophy and later strengthened by the pseudoscience of phrenology and intelligence based on brain size, it was proposed that people with black skin were biologically and intellectually different, therefore, inferior to white skinned people.

Quentin Tarantino's movie *Django Unchained* is a story about slavery in the United States. It stars Jamie Foxx and Leonardo DiCaprio and has a heart-stopping scene where the science of phrenology was used to prove that Blacks were anatomically built to be submissive and that phrenology not only explained inferiority, it justified slavery.

What's It Got To Do With Blackfullas In Australia?

On invasion, Aborigines were immediately judged by the British according to the global political and scientific racial trends of the times. White supremacy was entrenched within European culture and legitimised its own political domination using science as its master.

Australia inherited the Black inferiority/White superiority belief from the colonisers and it brought with it a legacy of terror, tragedy and trauma.

Brainwashing Strategy Number 1

GLORIFY A LIE THAT ONLY CERTAIN GROUPS OF PEOPLE WILL BENEFIT FROM

"No One Lives Here..."

Being labelled as sub-human and inferior because of our physical differences and morally inferior because we had no recognisable politics, leaders and religion, legitimised and strategically shaped the specific way in which the grandiose lie of 'terra nullius' (land belonging to no one) was used as a weapon to disregard Blackfulla sovereignty and eliminate the need to establish treaties and negotiate the purchasing of land.

Perhaps the inferiority status applied to Blackfullas was the reason that motivated Cook to disobey his instructions from King George III on what to do if he were to find that the land was inhabited. Perhaps the Brits expected to find white skinned Indigenous people here. How could the British possibly be expected to build good relationships and then negotiate land deals, which is what Cook was instructed to do, with Blacks who were by definition biologically inferior and were no more than animals?

Under British common law and property ownership, the land was considered uninhabited. Settlement was therefore asserted, rather than an invasion, and colonisation began.

McGrath (1995 p.1) emphasised this action of colonisation was out of step with other 'new world' countries such as North America, Canada and neighbouring New Zealand. The terra nullius decision legalised the invasion of Gadigal country and the Eora Nation, it authorised the theft of all Blackfulla lands and it justified the horrific means by which Blackfulla Nations throughout the continent were terrorised, overpowered and colonised.

To this day, in spite of the Mabo determination of the High Court in 1992 to overrule the legality of terra nullius, its legacy continues to negatively shape public opinion of, and political decisions regarding, First Nations peoples and the many social issues we now face as a result of this historic decision.

Brainwashing Strategy Number 2

REPEAT THE LIE UNTIL OTHERS START BELIEVING IT

"You Blacks Are Nothing But Animals..."

Sheehan (2012 p.81) explains that "racism was an essential tool of the colonial progress. Colonial racism is a highly ordered and well organised system for the elimination of Indigenous peoples." In early written records, First Nations peoples were referred to as anything but human. It was common to find language which described us as wild animals, apes, barbaric, primitive, native pests, savages and uncivilised, mere vermin.

"The habit of regarding the natives as vermin, to be cleared off the face of the earth, has given the average Queenslander a tone of brutality and cruelty in dealing with blacks. I have heard men of culture and refinement, of the greatest humanity and kindness to their fellow whites, and who when you meet them here at home you would pronounce to be incapable of such deeds, talk, not only of the wholesale butchery but of the individual murder of natives, exactly as they would talk of a day's sport, or having to kill some troublesome animal." (British High Commissioner, Arthur Hamilton Gordon, wrote privately to his friend William Gladstone, Prime Minister of England 1883 cited in Tatz).

Peter Cunningham, who was one of the first White men to receive a land grant in the Hunter Valley, supported the belief that the Kooris were not far removed from the ape. He wrote: *"How is it that the abject animal state in which they (Aborigines) live should place them at the very zero of civilisation, constituting in a measure the connecting link between man and the monkey tribe – for really some of the old women only seem to require a tail to complete the identity."* (Miller 1985 p. 25)

Such references dehumanised us even further and deepened the black inferiority/white superiority myth.

The Hon Linda Burney MP, former New South Wales Government Minister and current Deputy Leader of the NSW Opposition, remembered being taught as a 13-year-old that, *"My people were savages and the closest example to Stone Age man living today. I vividly recall wanting to turn into a piece of paper and slip quietly through the crack in the floor,"* she said. *"Growing up as an Aboriginal child, looking into the mirror of our country… your reflection was at best distorted and at worst non-existent."* (Sydney Morning Herald, Jonathan Pearlman and Joel Gibson May 23, 2007).

By the early 19th century, the black inferiority/white superiority belief was deeply entrenched within the Australian culture and psyche. Cunneen (2001) explains that, *"According to the social Darwinian view, Aborigines were the lowest rung on the evolutionary ladder, the most backward race of people in the world."*

By denying our intellect based on racist assumptions and philosophical and scientific theories, the British were able to deny our humanity and justify the brutal killing era of warfare and genocide that followed invasion.

Brainwashing Strategy Number 3

USE THE LIE TO DESTROY AND EXPLOIT PEOPLE

"Blackfulla Leaders Were Determined By Whitefellas..."

It was soon learnt that Blackfulla societies operated within very complex models of leadership in accordance with systems of tribal lore, Dreaming, ceremony, kinship, sacred knowledge, men's business and women's business. In any event, important decisions were largely made following a democratic system based on the consensus of the whole tribe.

The sophistication of this collective system of tribal leadership and governance was valued to ensure the well-being, spirituality and survival of the tribe. This system was in contradiction to much of the European-style of individual leadership. The British would often break Blackfulla cultural protocols when trying to identify one person being in charge of the tribe.

The very system of Blackfulla leadership, which once successfully maintained cultural harmony and balance, was a target point for the White man to destroy by all means possible and force an individualistic doctrine upon them.

Lachlan Macquarie, Governor of New South Wales in 1810, commenced a system of chieftainship for dealing with the friendly tribes. It meant that each tribe would now have a singular leader called a chief, king or queen who would be determined by Macquarie and later, others. It enabled the authorities to control who was and who was not a leader in accordance with the values and aims of colonial expansion and economic gain. It was a colonial strategy which was being used with success in North America. (National Museum of Australia website)

To help colonial authorities instantly recognise the tribe's chief or king, a symbol of leadership called a "breastplate" was worn around their necks. It was a metallic, often crescent-shaped, plate also known as a kingplate, brassplate or a gorget, decorated with motifs and the name and title of the person." (National Museum of Australia website).

"Whitefella historians suggest that the breastplate strategy had the well-meaning intention of trying to promote peaceful relationships between the Blacks and the colonisers." Perhaps it was. "Some tribes did indeed embrace this imposed model of leadership, whilst others saw it as another way of oppression." (National Museum of Australia website).

Blackfullas who were selected as acceptable leaders were expected to obey and help out with the colonial process in return for status and benefits for themselves and their tribes. Although Blackfullas were still considered an inferior race, their newly assigned leadership ranking immediately elevated them in the eyes of the European authorities and ensured their safety. Part of their leadership role included acting as an intermediary between the tribe and the government.

The breastplates were presented not only to perceived chiefs and faithful servants but later to Blackfullas as recognition for acts of bravery in helping Whites. This was evidenced by Pooinipun, Toompani, Woondu, Nu-Ah-Ju, Nuggun, Jackie Jackie and one other unnamed hero, who were my own Quandamooka Countrymen, when in 1847 they were rewarded by the Governor with brassplates and a fishing boat for rescuing sailors aboard the 'Sovereign' which sunk in Moreton Bay with only 10 survivors. (North Stradbroke Island Historical Museum).

This process of singling out friendly tribes, favouring and hand-picking certain Aborigines as leaders and distinguishing them with titles, breastplates and other benefits, most times was to ensure their conformity with the European's efforts to acquire their land without resistance, ignore their sovereignty and neglect the establishment of treaties. If Aborigines resisted, under the British Crown it was law that they could be shot.

The process was inherently debilitating as it contributed to breaking down the cultural and spiritual power bases of those tribes forced to participate. Knowing that we were considered 'less than' to the White man and that extreme acts of physical violence and psychological terror were used if we challenged our social status, riddled our Fullas with a consciousness of fear and compliance in order to stay alive.

Think about it: It served the colonisers well to use this divisive political strategy, it cleverly contributed to destroying Blackfulla models of lore and leadership, kept Blackfullas under surveillance by other Blackfullas, controlled Black resistance, discouraged the establishment of mutant leadership and it set our people up to be economically exploited. We would assert that the imposition of this breastplate leadership approach clearly demonstrated the deeply ingrained superior belief that, 'Whites know what is best for the Blacks.'

Thanks to a society structured to protect and expand White superiority, our capacity to think beyond survival and servitude has left us with a profound wound and impact on the 'leadership blueprint' we as Blackfullas try to operate from within today.

Consider that whilst we may be living in the 21st century, our minds are still in battle with the continuous paradox between "Blackfullas aren't as good as Whitefellas" and the drive and strive towards self-determination.

Brainwashing Strategy Number 4

INDUCE FEAR AND ANGER

"It's A Crime To Assert Your Blackfulla Leadership..."

Criminalisation was part of the British culture. Maybe it was in their blood. Their automatic response towards anyone who questioned, broke or resisted their rule was to criminalise and punish them. The tall ships were full of people who were testament to that.

In the last 40 years undeniable evidence such as Henry Reynolds (2013) book, *Forgotten Wars,* has surfaced to prove what we already knew to be true and has been written about by many Blackfulla historians, authors and academics. First Nations peoples went to war in defence of our Countries, in protection of our families, and in the preservation of our cultures. We have long resisted the horrific **processes** used by the colonisers to claim and colonise Australia.

Blackfulla resistance and leadership was criminalised the day Cook planted the Union Jack on Gadigal Country and claimed the entire continent for the British Empire. Reynolds (1995 ch.7) argues, "The popular view of the early nineteenth century of Aboriginal people as barbarous and treacherous savages, obscures the role that was played in the organised Indigenous struggle and later negotiations with colonial forces."

In short, we had next to no power to negotiate because we were not considered to be human beings.

Dr Watson (2012) says that from the outset the system had an embedded view that Aborigines were a backward race. There's always been this tendency to criminalise or use the criminal justice system as a way of dealing with Aboriginal peoples' differences. She calls it the 'deficit model of Aboriginality.'

Any of our men who had any remnant of a rebel spirit or asserted any signs of leadership were either killed immediately, kept under strict policing surveillance or tortured, usually to death.

John Pilger in his book, *The Secret Country: The First Australians Fight Back* (1985) tells stories of how it was common for Aboriginal men to have their penises cut off and they would run around screaming until they died.

A Black man was considered a danger to the establishment of colonial rule and therefore they had to be broken and controlled at all costs. His role as protector, provider and leader was taken from him and, by design, placed into the hands of White police. Blackfullas had no legal safeguards; we were considered an inferior race and were animalised.

All forms of resistance shown by Blackfullas against the process of colonisation were met with extreme policing measures of violence and force. This included turning a blind eye to racist policing practices and other Whites who committed crimes against Blacks. Johnston (1991a, vol.2, p14 cited in Cunneen 2001 p.53) explains that Native police and general police were granted the authority to 'quieten' Aboriginal people who resisted non-aboriginal rule.

In many areas, police were not maintaining law and order within the confines of the criminal law but rather were extending the reach of British jurisdiction over resisting Indigenous communities. For many Aboriginal people, the first contact they had with the police was with a paramilitary force of dispossession, dispensing summary justice and on some occasions they were involved in the indiscriminate massacre of clan and tribal groups (Cunneen 2001 p.50).

Our people were being criminalised for protecting their land, providing food for their families and for conducting restorative justice. Leaders and freedom/resistance fighters such as Dundalli, Pemulwuy, Windradyne, Nemarluk, Musquito, Yagan, the Kalkadoons, Tunnerminnerwait, Maulboyheenner and Jandamurra and many others, were revered by Blackfullas as resistance leaders but branded as savage murderers and criminals by the colonial system.

Whitefella laws were suspended when applied to Blacks. This enabled Blackfullas to be hunted down by the authorities and the native police or mounted police. Punishment included being shot dead on sight, shot and being captured, tried and publicly executed in front of Aborigines and then their bodies hung in trees as a collective punishment and warning to others (Cunneen 2001 p 60-61).

It was also common for resistance leaders to have their heads cut off and collected as trophies or studied under the pseudo-science of phrenology with the purpose of gaining further evidence of our inferiority. Many Blackfulla heads were sent to England, as was the case with Pemulwuy whose head to this day has never been found in any British repository. (Behrendt 2012 p 87 -89).

One sorry story is the account of Bennelong who was an Aboriginal warrior of the Wangal clan and a prominent leader in the Eora Nation's political and cultural life. Bennelong was kidnapped by Arthur Phillip and taken to Sydney Cove in 1789 as part of Phillip's plan to learn the language and customs of the local Aborigines. In spite of being kidnapped, Bennelong established a workable ambassadorial relationship with Phillip and the Crown.

On Bennelong's death in 1813, his obituary in the Sydney Gazette was unflattering, insisting that "…*he was a thorough savage, not to be warped from the form and character that nature gave him…*" (Wikipedia).

How very sad to think that, in spite of Bennelong's leadership in both his Aboriginal world and within the White colonial world, on his death he was still regarded by White society as nothing but a mere savage.

In the 1950s a new group of First Nations leaders was emerging in their own fields of expertise and who were revered by both Whites and Blacks. This included people such as Albert Namatjira, Douglas Grant, Harold Blair, David Unaipon, Harry Penrith, Doug Nicholls, Reg Saunders and others. All of these important figures of the 1950s were appropriated, exploited and renowned by state and federal governmental authorities in Aboriginal Affairs as being exemplars and success stories of the assimilation policy and yet, nearly every one of them grew up on segregated missions and reserves (Ramsland & Mooney 2012).

Despite having the SNL pushed in their face 24/7 and experiencing vicious racism, some criminalisation and ASIO investigations, all were successful and remained resilient and strong in their identity as First Nations peoples.

What is perhaps most memorable about these leaders is that the mainstream media showed a kindness towards them which was mighty unusual for the times.

'A Plea for the Australian Aborigines' was an article written in the *Sydney Mail* in 1917 about Pastor David Unaipon and Sergeant Douglas Grant. It was set out to debunk the popular notions held in White Australia that Aborigines lacked intelligence or had inferior intelligence to the Europeans and could not be educated in the European way.

For the times, it was almost a radical position to take. It read: *The Australian aborigine is not generally credited with the possession of much intelligence. We have been told that he represents the lowest type of man in the globe. Give a dog a bad name and it sticks. I want to try and remove the idea that the aborigine is incapable of being educated by giving a few instances that prove the fallacy of that contention."* (Ramsland & Mooney 2012 p.1-2)

Our resistance leaders of the 18th and 19th centuries became our activist leaders of the 60s and 70s who played an instrumental role in the establishment and the sacred business of the 1972 Aboriginal Tent Embassy. Included were Bertie Williams, Michael Anderson, Tony Coorey, Billy Craigie, Gary Foley, Bruce McGuinness, Roberta Sykes, Chicka Dixon, Charles Perkins, Kevin Gilbert, Barrie Dexter, Paul Coe, Dennis Walker, Sam Watson, Burnum Burnum, Harold Thomas, (Foley, Schaap & Howell 2014) and many, many well-deserving others.

"The mission has come to town," was one of my Uncle John Newfong's (Chief Spokesman and Media Coordinator for the Embassy 1972) funniest, yet most profound, sayings as he shared stories with us about the political influence and impact the Aboriginal Tent Embassy had. He always captivated us with his stories of how the Embassy inspired and moved Blackfullas from right across the country to come together in unity and leadership. He would laugh with fondness when he talked about how people piled into buses and cars and came from the bush, the outback,

from missions and reserves to Parliament House in Canberra to show support for the Aboriginal Tent Embassy and land rights.

The Aboriginal Tent Embassy woke Australia up again to the issues which were impacting First Nations peoples, and it ignited a flame of collective political activism that put land rights and sovereignty back on the government's agenda.

Like other leaders before them, they faced paramilitary force and violence when the police came in the first time to remove the tents and break up the peaceful protest. The government of the day had brought a new ordinance into effect which allowed them to do this. *"The paddy wagon...was parked on the gravel. The coppers opened the back... just threw them in.... The tents were ripped from the lawns and taken away in a police vehicle. Eight people, including five Aborigines, were arrested, while 'almost every demonstrator ringing the tent was injured or bruised in some way."* (Tribune, 1972: Canberra News 1972, cited in Foley, Schaap & Howell 2014).

This is a snap shot of the Aboriginal Tent Embassy. Other examples, such as the 1957 Palm Island Strike and the slippery injustice that followed the death in custody of a young Palm Islander Mulrunji Doomadgee in 2004, are further illustrations of where the shared leadership of Blackfullas plight against the injustices caused by the SNL has been met with violence by political and policing authorities.

In more recent times, our men and their families and community leadership has come into question with the Northern Territory Intervention (2001, July 28th, Witness The Intervention film). Wes Miller of the Jawoyn Association in the Beswick community in the Northern Territory said that, *"Since the intervention, many of the men felt as if they had done something wrong, like they were criminals. They were being branded wife bashers, child molesters, drunks and all those stereotypical tags. They felt like they weren't very good parents."*

Conway Bush said, *"I feel insulted, makes me feel like I've never been a parent. Makes me feel bad. I suffer from depression and I got to stay positive at all times because if I break down my kids break down, and the kids won't get an education if I can't perform as a parent and put food on the table, clothes on their backs and make them happy. Worst part is going to town with my wife to do the shopping and people look at you sideways thinking, "I wonder if he's a paedophile that Blackfulla over there."* (2001, July 28th, Witness The Intervention film)

Dehumanisation, racism, criminalisation, displacement, oppression, institutionalisation and exclusion are not the elements with which you build a strong model of leadership.

For generations, our people have lived within models of leadership where White superiority ruled with the bible in one hand and a gun in the other.

Brainwashing Strategy Number 5

TRAIN PEOPLE TO THINK AND BELIEVE THEY ARE WORTHLESS

"Ya Nothing But A Dumb Blackfulla And That's All You'll Ever Be"

The science of eugenics, together with the social Darwinist notion that the un-fittest don't survive, strongly influenced public opinions and protection-ist policies. It was believed that the 'full-blood' Aborigines would soon die out or eventually be bred out.

However, this was not the case. Cunneen (2001 p.63) explains that, *"By the turn of the century the growing 'half-caste' population was becoming a key problem in Aboriginal affairs."*

During most of the 20th century, policies of protection and assimilation were formalised to give legislative power to White governments and local authorities to legally:

1. Define who was and who was not a *real* Aborigine; and
2. Determine how they were to be treated and what quality of life they would have.

It was thought that this was a way of stopping the 'half-caste problem' from expanding and saving and civilising those who were categorised as 'half-caste' into White culture where they had a better chance of survival, becoming White, blending in and having the Blackfulla bred out of them.

Behrendt (2012) explains that the forcible removal of generations of Aboriginal and Torres Strait Islander children and babies from their fami-lies was a key strategy of the Assimilation policy. Today, these adults are known as the Stolen Generation. Sheehan (2012 p. 37) says, the experi-ences of the Stolen Generations people was racially motivated and their removal was part of a general and popular social, political and administra-tive regime aimed at reforming their innate (racial) deficiencies.

Some Whites believed and preached the theory that light-skinned Blacks were intellectually superior because they had some White blood in them. If an Aborigine was born a 'half-caste', had lighter coloured skin and looked like a White person they were more likely to be adopted or fostered into private respectable White homes and given White names. These children were more likely to be educated in a Whitefella school.

If they did well academically and were socially fitting in, it was because they were being raised by good White, Christian people. If the children struggled academically or played up at school and were becoming a handful at home, it was the 'Abo' coming out in them and most often they were sent back to an institution. Many of these children grew up not knowing they were Indigenous until they became adults.

If a child was born a 'full-blood' Aborigine or had darker coloured skin and looked to be a 'full-blood' Aborigine, they were branded as even more inferior than the 'half-caste' children. These children were more likely to be sent to a highly controlled, segregated training institution or out to work. They were excluded from going to a White school and their level of education was very basic, mostly focusing on training the girls to be domestic servants for middle-class White families and the boys to be labourers once they left the institutions.

There was no encouragement or expectation for these children to complete school or aim to do anything other than manual and domestic work.

Generations of Aborigines and Torres Strait Islanders had it drummed into them that they were worthless, had no brains, and wouldn't amount to anything but being a slave to the White man. School curriculum and teaching practices were expected to attack the lifestyle and intelligence of the Aborigines and Torres Strait Islanders.

Education and religion were instrumental in embedding these beliefs of inferiority. *"If people are brainwashed to think they're inferior, then people begin to act in negative ways and this is served up as proof of 'inferiority' This gets handed down to our kids who hear it all around."* (A workshop participant quoted in S Gorringe, J Ross and C Fforde's, *Will the real Aborigine Please Stand Up: Strategies for breaking the stereotypes and changing the conversations* AIATSIS Research Discussion Paper 28).

The stripping away of generations of Blackfulla lore, culture, families, language and identity forced many of our peoples to be indoctrinated with the idea that perhaps we were in fact, inferior and not at all capable of being White-way civilised and educated. Instead, we were the property of the Crown. Property to be stolen, bought, kidnapped, traded, sold, inherited, used, abused and disposed of... For the White man this was "business as usual".

Brainwashing Strategy Number 6

DIVIDE AND CONQUER

"You're More Intelligent Than Those Blacks 'Cause You Got Some White Blood In Ya!"

Such discriminatory categorising and the wounding and pain caused by segregating generations of our families into categories of value and inferiority according to our physical features and the colour of our skin, really screwed up our identity. It caused a profound sense of confusion and powerlessness and destroyed our sense of belonging.

Regardless of their skin colour, children were programmatically stripped of their cultural identity and brainwashed into a mindset of Black inferiority as they were taught to reject and fear their own culture and Aboriginality. Inducing people with fear and anger makes it harder for people to think logically because it keeps them locked into a state of anxiety and panic and a sense of '*I have to survive at all costs.*'

Sheehan (2012 p.38) reports that in dormitories, lighter-skinned Aboriginal children were often taught to fear Aboriginal people; a tactic that created barriers, locking many into mindsets that divided them from their families. Burgmann (2003 Chapter 2 pp 44-97) continues, *"White people believed that they were superior to us and that if we had some White racial mixture, we were better than those Koories who had a very dark colouring... For a while some of us were convinced that to be Black or dark was to be inferior."*

Many fair-skinned children who were forced into dormitories were treated terribly by darker-skinned Aborigines and adults. (Bringing Them Home Report 1997 Ch. 5 Penny, Murray and Trevor's Story of being sent to Palm Island). Anti-Aboriginal propaganda within the foster homes was a powerful weapon in stopping Aboriginal socialisation, as the children were often taught that Blacks on the reserves were corrupt, sinful and dirty.

As a result of this constant ideological repression, many girls became embarrassed at the colour of their skin. They would cross the road in order to avoid an Aboriginal man, just because in the end, they themselves had come to believe that he was a threat – dirty, brutal, and Black. Bell Hooks (Burrell 2010 p 217) explains that, *"Often Black people in such settings collude in their own shaming and humiliation because they have been socialised by internalised racism to feel 'chosen,' and better than other Black people.*

> **Internalised racism is like a terminal illness and can be a long, slow death.**

We have always been known as the 'black problem' which Whitefullas have to fix. Throughout history, our identity has been constantly redefined according to the advancement of White Australia's economic, political and social status. What remained constant, however, was our perceived inferiority and the simultaneous use of physical and political exclusion and violence by White people to force their superiority upon us and keep us in our place.

"I was not born with an inferiority complex. I did not acquire one. I had one forced upon me and was made (by law) to accept this complex as my just lot." (Cooper 1968, cited in WCC 1971, cited in Pattel-Gray 1989 p.41).

Indoctrination using labels strengthened the SNL and planted the festering seeds for our people to internalise their pain and suffering and eventually to take it out on each other. *"The damage and trauma past policies caused is still being felt every day by Aboriginal people. They would internalise their grief, guilt and confusion and inflict further pain on themselves and others around them."* (Secretariat of the National Aboriginal and Islander Child Care organisations, cited in Tatz 1999).

Today, these festering seeds of inadequacies and "identity conflict" (Miller 2012 p.58) have manifested as lateral violence which is now occurring at epidemic rates in many First Nations communities.

Our peoples have been programmed not to recognise the complexities of the SNL and are automatically drawn into playing the lateral violence game.

I have been both a victim and a perpetrator of lateral violence. In 1996 I was part of an Indigenous Education Executive Development program aimed at training First Nations educators who had the potential and passion to move into leadership positions within education in Queensland.

I had great mentors around me, both black and white fullas, and as much as I loved the work and was 100% committed to educational excellence for our kids and their families, there were times when I felt completely inadequate amongst the other distinguished members who were participants of the Executive Development program.

It was the first time I had worked in such a high level environment and, as much as I wanted it, I was scared I wasn't good enough and that I would fail.

There was no way in hell I was going to let anyone else know how I was feeling so to cover it up I acted super-confident, like I knew it all and was better than anyone else, especially around White staff and colleagues.

Yes, I took on an air of self-appointed superiority, whilst pretending I wasn't.

I would often find myself gossiping about, or running down, other Blackfulla colleagues and professionals – just to make myself feel better, which really didn't last very long.

Fortunately I hit a brick wall before I did too much damage to others. Thankfully the experience made me grow up quickly and reconnected me with my old ancestral people who started me on my journey of inner healing.

Gosh, it really woke me up to realise how the SNL caused my identity to become fractured between who I was as a Quandamooka Goori, and who I thought I had to become to 'make it' in the White man's world. Living in two worlds during that stage of my life was hard work.

It literally almost killed me – more about that in Chapter 8, *Find Out How Your BS Shapes Your Life*.

If you were to think I was suffering from the 'Black crab syndrome,' you would be right. The Black crab syndrome is where you've got a bucket full of crabs and each time one crab climbs to the top of the bucket to seek its freedom, the other crabs pull it back down again. Mind you, it could be because the other crabs don't like being stepped all over so some crabs can get to the top first and rather than give them a hand up and a hand out of the bucket, they're pulled back down into the bucket with the rest of the crabs.

I was the Black crab pulling everyone else down and then expecting them to give me a hand up.

This is one example of lateral violence. Lateral violence is where we take our own suffering out on other people. STARS believes there is also an "inner violence" which is where we take our pain out on ourselves.

At this period in my life I wanted so much to belong and yet I felt like such an outsider. I had internalised years of historical oppression and perceptions that to be a Blackfulla was to be dysfunctional and disadvantaged. The limited strategy I had at the time to cope and ease the pain of my own insecurities, was to take it out on my own mob.

Whatever you want to call this type of mindset and behaviour, it successfully reinforces the existing negative perceptions and validates the stereotypes of our inferior status.

It might sound funny reading it here, but hear this: it is part of that whole inter-generational cycle of being brainwashed to think we're not good enough. Consider that our silent thinking has become such that, if we can't be as good as the White man, then let us compete with being better than our black sisters and brothers.

Ouch!

Brainwashing Strategy Number 7

KEEP PEOPLE DEPENDENT

"We Know What's Best For You!"

To control Blackfullas and uphold a structure of racial superiority, it was vital to block all pathways to accessing the ability to think and reason for ourselves. Poor or no education, racist media campaigns, limited employment, poverty, institutionalisation and other psychological boundaries were put in place to convince us of our own inferiority and implanted emotions of worthlessness and helplessness.

Our ignorance was necessary to maintain colonial security and for the machination of assimilation to take place.

The failure of successive governments to acknowledge our human rights and assure our safety solidified and legitimised levels of tremendous personal and cultural insecurity. Life's uncertainty and brutality conditioned us to become reliant on the very people and systems which oppressed us.

Consider that we might continue to share a colonial relationship with the government and its systems which are, by historical design, geared to keep us psychologically dependent, socially impotent, economically dispossessed, politically marginalised and culturally exhausted. It is almost like we are spiritually imprisoned waiting for others to liberate us.

This is also one of the impacts of a welfare system that regards Blackfullas as "the problem" and not being part of the solution. It goes beyond providing a safety net and a "hand up and hand out' – it actually sucks the life force and confidence that "I can do it," from individuals.

The reality is that we have always been at the bottom of every good list going and at the top of every bad list. We have been identified as Australia's most disadvantaged group according to all socio-economic indicators (Human rights Law Centre 2011).

Consider that whilst we hold this title we are kept on the political agenda and some might say this is a good thing because, granted, it has raised the consciousness of Australians to the rights, issues and injustices of us Fullas. It has served to bring about collective social movements, royal commissions, policy changes, inquiries, resources and money etc.

However, the paradox is that the label of 'disadvantage' is premised on deficiency and weakness. It shouts out loud with subliminal messages that to be a First Nations person includes taking on the identity of 'disadvantage'.

'Disadvantage' psychologically embeds a message that being Black is somehow equivalent to failure, wrongness, badness and burdensome.

Here is another catch. Once again authorities are telling us who we are and who we have to be. Consider that this very process of brainwashing alone makes it highly probable that we will produce the results that are aligned with the label. It is a universal law of quantum physics that what you focus on will expand.

The continued identification and campaigning for Blackfullas to be disadvantaged successfully reaffirms our inferior status.

We are led down the funnel of the well-oiled self-generating machine of the inferiority model of Blackness, keeping the SNL safe and secretly in place.

What if the result is that we remain inferior and keep on underachieving in exchange for acknowledgement, facilities, money and resources and the employment of White (and yes some Black) experts to help fix our problems?

The system is geared towards rewarding Blackness as a deficit and whether we like it or not, we are caught within the paradigm of inferiority.

Black disadvantage is premised on welfare colonialism and it is a huge money-making business and has been so for both Whitefellas, and in more recent times some of us Blackfullas.

However, contrary to populist political propaganda from people like Pauline Hanson, former leader of the One Nation Party (Maiden Speech 1996), those who have financially benefitted the most from our disadvantaged label are not us Blackfullas. Rather, the beneficiaries of the big dollar funding are predominantly non-Indigenous bureaucrats who are employed to design the policies and administer, manage and lead the programs and projects.

Think about it.

If we were really the recipients of ALL those billions of dollars over the years, isn't there a good chance all us Blackfullas and our communities would be doing proper well right now? Wouldn't the socio-economic gap between First Nations peoples and non-Indigenous Aussies be much smaller, perhaps even non-existent? Wouldn't we be living well into our 80s and 90s and in darn good health?

Cronin (2007 p.199 cited in Moreton-Robinson) explains that, *"Welfare colonialism benefited governments, private enterprise and ultimately the Australian people because benefits accrued from the exploitation of Indigenous land, labour and money. Governments of all levels, private enterprise, and the Australian people as a whole, have not yet had an interest in the long-term social and economic viability of Indigenous communities or in addressing post-colonial issues with Indigenous people. Welfare colonialism also necessitated the creation of bureaucratic structures and institutions that control and manage the lives and affairs of indigenous people and communities."*

He singles out a number of industries that make their living and accumulate profits from the existence of the Indigenous welfare economy: the government and service delivery industries, the goods and services industry, for example stores and pubs. Now add to the list builders and telecommunications and the consulting, professional and academic industries as represented by lawyers, anthropologists, planners, policy-makers, researchers, academics and so on (Cronin 2007 cited in Moreton-Robinson).

In the 2014 6th Annual *Closing the Gap* Report which focuses on addressing Indigenous disadvantage, the statistics tell the story. In the seven years since the launch of the campaign, the current results are showing that the campaign is failing and in the words of Prime Minister Abbott, *"We are not on track to achieve the more important and the more meaningful targets."*

In fact, in the area of employment, the gap has gotten bigger and, disturbingly, in health Blackfullas are still dying on average ten years before non-Indigenous people.

Obviously, something is still not working after seven years.

So, whilst a majority of the money invested in the 'Blackfulla industry' since the 1970s continues to not produce the results and make quantifiable returns on the investment, money still continues to be generated back into the system which created the problems in the first place.

> It is a vicious psychological cycle of co-dependency… and the very thing it counts on for its existence is to ensure that people believe that *Blackfullas are not as good as Whitefellas*, that Blackfullas can't control their own affairs and that Blackfullas will always need non-Indigenous people to lead the way in fixing their problems.

What if the games of protectionism and assimilation have not become extinct, what if the ringmasters have just developed other language and skills…?

Brainwashing Strategy Number 8

CONTROL WHAT PEOPLE WATCH AND READ

"Look At All The Good Things We Have Done To Help These Poor Blackfullas"

As a nation in the last 40+ years, we have celebrated milestones such as Australia's endorsement of the United Nations Declaration on the Rights of Indigenous Peoples, the Mabo Decision, the Walk for Reconciliation over the Sydney Harbour Bridge, and The Apology. We can't help but wonder if these opportunities have also been used as political symbols and tools to lull Australians into a false sense of patriotic optimism and actually moved attention away from the rights of First Nations peoples.

Let's face it. No one wants to be confronted with truths that challenge us to reflect on our values, beliefs and identities. As you will learn in later chapters, this literally freaks your brain out.

Consider that as a nation we have been persuaded to believe that racism no longer exists or it's not as bad as it used to be and that we should all be very proud that regardless of our race or our blemished history we can all share a beer and a pie at the footy because we are all now on an equal footing. "She'll be right Mate." It's the Ozzie way to let bygones be bygones and walk as one, hand in hand, into a new and brighter national future.

John Howard played this card beautifully during his 11 year term as Prime Minster. He tapped into the patriotism gland of the voting public and with strategic media campaigning sold the public a romanticised story of nationalism with sprinklings of assimilation. Howard (2005) said, *"I do not accept that there is underlying racism in this country"*. He used the agenda of practical reconciliation to espouse his views on how history ought to focus on the positive achievements of the good Australian olden times of settlement and taming the country and not focus on all the bad colonial stuff that had to do with the 'I' word – Invasion, killing Blacks and taking their land and children away.

Howard was of the view that history should not make the generations of today feel guilty and accountable for the errors and misdeeds of earlier generations. The pendulum had swung too far...

The interesting thing about Howard's position on history is that this is the way Australia's history has always been presented. It is predominantly told by White historians and anthropologists and espouses the values and beliefs and stories of predominantly White Australians.

What does remain constant however, within both the black and white narratives of history, is the indisputable evidence that white colonialists believed that '*Blackfullas weren't as good as Whitefellas*' and it was used as the glue which bound and permitted the unjust ways colonisation happened in this country.

Prime Minster Howard's refusal to say sorry to the Stolen Generation, his rejection of many of the inquiry's findings and conclusions in vital reports such as the *Bringing them Home* report and *The Little Children are Sacred* report, and his decision, known as the Intervention, to send the army into the Northern Territory to protect the children, is the kind of political manoeuvring which works to successfully keep Australians officially ignorant and incapable of hearing this SNL, and feeling its consequences.

It enables the continuation of the lie to lurk just beneath the surface of people's consciousness.

In short, we have all – black and white – been brainwashed!

Make no mistakes, the SNL has collectively wounded each of us and it has taken on a slippery intelligence of its own. We have iced-over the trauma it has caused for all Australians for centuries.

Let us make this very clear, it is not just a Blackfulla problem, this SNL is a human being problem.

As you read the book you will become aware of how this lie continues to impact how you lead your life and how your life directs your leadership.

We are at a very unique time in history right now!

There is a collective group of Blackfulla 'brainiacs' who, although they may be divided in their thinking and ideologies, Vicki and I believe are united in their undying love for and their commitment to making a real difference in the daily lives of their families, their communities and for all Australians.

Collectively they have the history, the intellect, the skill sets, the political nuance, the networks, the creative power, spiritual intelligence, the access to resources and the wit and tenacity needed and required to lead a very new-looking social movement.

We need these leaders, and leaders like you, to begin grooming our youth.

There are now more black faces in white places such as the parliaments of Australia, the medical and legal worlds, within the corporate business sector, and public sector agencies throughout the country.

There is much more open goodwill and activism from non-indigenous folks, and more companies and organisations declaring their commitment and contributions to a united Australia by developing reconciliation action plans aimed at developing relationships, showing respect and increasing opportunities for Aboriginal and Torres Strait Islander peoples.

We now have immediate access to modern technology, entry to influential international platforms, and more Blackfullas moving into positions of power and authority within the mainstream which can make a difference.

We are now at a time when the opportunity for moving ahead as a collective voice has never been greater.

What else is possible?

We do believe that if we can seize this moment and step up into a new era of Blackfulla leadership, forge our own paths for healing and begin de-colonising our own thinking, then we predict new sustainable results will follow.

Let us not forget that we have used our skills and expertise to survive for the last 200+ years, and those same skills and expertise, if used in new ways, can empower us to move from surviving to thriving.

If you really want to transform areas of your life and improve the results you are getting as a strong, smart, Blackfulla leader, then you need to consider where this SNL, *"Blackfullas aren't as good as Whitefellas,"* has an indistinguishable hold on your full potential and your future.

The truth shall set you free.....

It is hoped that this book will support and empower you in your journey to begin unlearning and breaking free from the constraints of continued racism and the malevolence of the lie that *Blackfullas aren't as good as Whitefellas*!

Your time is NOW!

"Life is not about 'you get what you're given.' Life is about 'you get what you choose!'

Nicole Watego-Gilsenan

CHAPTER 4

Announcing… A New Era Of Blackfulla Leadership

How are you feeling after reading the first three chapters? When we take a look at the history it is a thoughtful reminder of the considerable progress we have made as Blackfullas and a sobering wake-up call for how much work remains to be done.

Now, for crying out loud, don't go falling victim to the '*woe is me*' trap or '*if it weren't for those bloody Whitefellas*' trap or '*my Mob make me shame*' trap, that is exactly what the SNL feeds on to give it power and velocity.

This is not about pointing the finger at White Australia or being a victim or being a victim kicker. If we are honest with ourselves, we have all "been there done that" at some stage and we know it doesn't work and makes us feel rotten. If we continue playing into the entanglement of these games we achieve three things:

1. Everyone is a loser,
2. The games work as a mechanism to keep the SNL firmly and silently in place,
3. These games will eventually kill us!

This chapter, along with the remaining part of this book, is intended to hand responsibility over to you so that you can start the critical thinking that needs to come with de-colonising your psyche, re-opening and getting rid of the internal mind clutter that has been built up over time because of the SNL. Once this de-cluttering process starts and you gain momentum, you will notice new spaces of thought and possibilities will begin to open up for you.

> **You will become aware that we do have the power to choose and choose wisely!**

This is super exciting, we have two choices. When we look at the complexities of our history we can either choose to become a victim of it and feed addictive emotional pathologies which isn't wrong or bad, it just limits us and makes us sick or we can use history to enliven our victorious spirit, call forth the wisdom of the ages to affirm our identity, strengthen our intellectual integrity and build psychological resilience.

It is from this sacred space that we believe you tap into your Ancestral powers, your creative juices get turned on and you're powered up to begin creating a new vision for the future. A vision which infuses you and others with inspiration, hope and distinction, pulling you like an invisible magnetic force into a shared future.

Blackfullas Leading Whitefella Style...

The SNL cleverly programs people to believe that Blackfulla leadership has to look a certain way in order for us to 'make it' in the mainstream. As Annette (Graduate from 2013 Dada Gana National Women's Leadership Program) says, *"We have to do leadership the White man's way or the highway."* This puts enormous pressure on us, regardless if we come from a rural, remote or urban area.

Is this assimilation-ism done with the purpose of us Fullas giving up what we know works for us Mob and then taking on Whitefella models of leadership and the values, beliefs, language and practices that go with it? It seems the more senior we get as an individual, or advanced as a community, the more compliance to the "mainstream" model is expected.

Perhaps this is an unspoken rule. I have never found it in any job description or written in a code of conduct book anywhere. Is it a secret rule that we must learn and follow if we want access into the upper echelons of Whitefella influence and decision-making power and entry into the VIB (Very Important Blackfulla) club?

The conflict is that these expectations may not always align with, or positively support, our identity and cultural ways of doing leadership business. Australia likes to roll out stories about the rise of prominent leaders in Aboriginal and Torres Strait Islander communities to reaffirm its '*Land of a Fair Go*' mentality, but it hides the fact that many more potential Blackfulla leaders decide to leave leadership roles faster than you can say, "see ya later alligator", never to be seen or heard from again.

Many of our Mob don't even know that they have the choice to choose a different model of leadership other than the one they have been conditioned to believe and operate within.

What is interesting is the responses we get when we have asked people in our programs, "*What models of Blackfulla leadership do you operate from?*" Most times they stare at us like we've got two heads and then wait for us to give them an answer, or hand them a framework.

Whilst their reaction may be valid, it amplifies how dependent we have become on others to give us answers and solutions to challenges and problems that only we can truly solve.

Consider that the SNL brainwashing project of 1788 continues to be effective. If we get real with ourselves then we need to acknowledge that we too have been caught up in its hypnotic spell, dulling our capacity to be self-reflective, keeping our hearts shut down and our minds boxed in.

Let's start to unpack how the past has contributed to who you are and your views on leadership. Answer the following questions and then reflect on your answers.

1. How do you think the history of the SNL has influenced the current ways in which First Nations peoples lead?
2. How effective are these leadership models in the 21st century?
3. How do you think these current models of leadership have contributed to your style of leadership?
4. What is your philosophy on leadership?
5. What expectations do you have for yourself?

Thank you for taking the time to answer these questions. As we said in the introduction we encourage you to use the book as a living resource.

So, what did you learn about yourself and your leadership by answering the five questions? This simple task gives you a snapshot of how history is a strong determinant for shaping who we are right now, and some would think a good predictor for who we become in the future. Or is it?

As you continue through the book you will get present to just how much freedom and power you have in self-determining the direction of your life and your leadership.

In the following chapter you will begin to examine how the past plays a significant role in shaping your current leadership blueprint and defining who you are as a leader.

Let's briefly look at one modern day belief born as a result of the SNL that psychologically continues to enslave us. It has been passed down through the generations and was originally well intentioned to make possible our social and economic advancement. It sounds something like this.... *"Blackfullas have to work harder, work longer and do better than a White person if they want to get ahead."* Sound familiar?

Perhaps the advice isn't completely off the mark but if that's all it takes, certainly many of us ought to be much further along and our communities should be healthy and happy places. This cloaked competitiveness however, has become ingrained in our 'Beingness' and now it doesn't just refer to Blackfullas doing better than the White man this new-aged competitiveness has us competing with each other, including our families.

Whilst competitiveness is not wrong and certainly may warrant a place in a new era of Blackfulla leadership, in its current form it has a self-defeating habit of diverting attention away from co-operation, consultation, compassion, cohesion and community. As an Aunty from the Gold Coast said at the Social and Emotional Wellbeing (SEWB) Queensland conference in 2013, *"We are now competing with our family when apply-ing for grants. The funding bodies now give the money to the organisa-tions that have the best submission writers, not the organisations who have the greatest need."*

In the last three decades the belief in working hard and getting a good mainstream education or training was hailed as one keystone of suc-cess. But the world is changing and now evolving at great speeds, and today these strategies simply aren't enough. If we cling to old beliefs that worked in the past, without taking into account how the world is shifting, we will likely feel frustrated and boxed in, or worse, lose our vision for the future we want.

To move forward, we believe we must now begin to redefine what Blackfulla leadership in the 21st century means, firstly to us as indiv-iduals and then as a collective group.

> **We must discern what core values, ideologies, and beliefs we are currently operating from and review whether or not they are working for us, or against us.**

While we have made tremendous progress, we still face tremendous challenges, and tremendous work remains to be done. Our communities and our country cannot afford to wait.

For generations, the social programming of expected failure has played an instrumental role in crafting the modern day mentality of a no-to-low expectation of success for Blackfullas. As a nation we are now up against an epidemic of the indisputable evidence supporting how the building of this low-expectation mindset for First Nations peoples is now being fulfilled and impacting all Australians:

- Low educational outcomes
- Low levels of sustained employment
- Low number of people who own their own homes
- Low levels of good health and well-being
- Low levels of economic independence
- Low numbers of people in Federal and State Parliaments
- Low numbers of people in mainstream media
- Low numbers of people running their own successful business
- Low numbers of people living beyond 70 years of age

If, as leaders, we are going to provide real value to the lives of our communities, we need to be first in line when it comes to asking – and answering for ourselves – the hard core questions.

Two questions which are vital for us all to answer before authentic change can occur are:

1. *How is who I am being and what I am doing, perpetuating the SNL?*

2. *What am I responsible for which is contributing to the norm of low expectations and disadvantage?*

Critical questions such as these need to be asked, and we need to dig deep and answer them honestly. What value do you think answering these two questions will have on shaping you as a leader?

Try it and see....

Short Term "Benefits" of the SNL for Blackfullas...

Consider that given the ever-changing demands placed upon us now in the workplace, a hint of the good old Ozzie, *'She'll be right mate'* attitude, aka the *'close enough is good enough'* attitude, is beginning to creep into our work ethic. The SNL loves this slackness of attitude as it enables us to make excuses to not work to our full leadership potential, dumb ourselves down, withhold our greatness, and then not expect it in others. This tends to activate our own doubts and low expectations, it reinforces harmful stereotypes and has us tolerating and justifying our own poor behaviour and that of others.

This includes simple things like not keeping people accountable to deadlines and then blaming them for not so great outcomes; employing or keeping people employed when they lack the skill level required to do the job; ignoring racism and staff complaints; providing staff with lots of feel-good stuff on their performance reviews and evaluations but avoiding providing them with correction and further training when required; ignoring it when staff show up late for work, take too long for lunch or cigarette breaks; or purposefully break the proper protocols of cultural business and Sorry business in order to take time off work.

The compounding of little things like this perpetuates a big message of low expectations and will, without fail, successfully train people in how to become dependent and under-achievers. In the end, the 'She'll be right mate' attitude will have you feeling depleted as a leader, make the workplace unpredictable and hell, break down a sense of trust and safety, stop good work and outcomes being achieved, staff ending up resenting you, fighting with each other..... and then they quit, or you get out first.

To the uneducated public this screams out the message, "Blackfullas can't lead in and manage their own affairs," re-delivering the message that Whitefellas are better than Blackfullas.

Why don't you see if you have been influenced by the SNL and the 'She'll be right mate' attitude? Answer the five questions.

TASK

1. Write down any self-defeating beliefs and attitudes that you have and which you have tolerated.

_____

_____

_____

2. How has this impacted your leadership?

_____

_____

_____

3. Write down as many examples as you can think of where you know you have been slack and made excuses for it.

_____

_____

_____

4. How has this impacted your confidence and self-esteem?

_____

_____

_____

5. How do you think this has influenced the way you have made decisions?

_____

_____

_____

Short Term "Benefits" of the SNL for Whitefellas…

This ugly lie that "Blackfullas are not as good as Whitefellas" enables White people to not confront their own racism and paternalism. It's fair to say that the average White Australian has not been schooled in Australia's black history and finds it hard to relate to a First Nations person outside of the stereotypes they have been conditioned to believe and expect.

Sadly, many White people know how to relate to and treat a First Nations person who has dark skin, who has little education, is unemployed and likes the grog. That fits the inter-generational image they have grown up believing in.

What many Whitefellas get challenged by, especially in a professional working environment, is how to '*be with*' a Blackfulla who is well accomplished, highly articulate and educated, holds degrees or is well schooled from experience, is in a position of authority and may in fact be more qualified than they are and make more money than they do or may be fair skinned.

This can be very confronting to the subconsciousness of superiority locked within the identity of Whiteness.

In the leadership and healing work we do at STARS Institute we find that all the Whitefellas we've worked with genuinely want to, or do already, share positive relationships with First Nations peoples. They are active in their commitments to building a greater understanding of our history and issues, they're advocates of human rights and social justice and they are good people. Their souls are hurting too and in their hearts they know what is right and just and they're committed to wanting to make a difference.

This is not yet the case with much of non-Indigenous Australia. The 2012 Barometer reveals that for many Australians, "*As much as we want to think having great relationships between Blackfullas and non-Indigenous Aussies is a good idea, in a nutshell, the results reveal that currently our relationships are very poor, that there are high levels of prejudice between us and that we don't trust each other."*

You can hear how embedded the SNL is when people (Black and White) start asking questions and making statements which try to define our identity and fit us back into the stereotypes perpetuated by the SNL. It may sound like:

1. Are your qualifications real or did you have to do a special course?
2. I'm not racist but...
3. You speak really well.
4. You're too white to be a real Blackfulla.
5. Why should I say sorry, I wasn't even around when all that bad stuff went down?
6. Are you qualified to work only with Aboriginal and Torres Strait Islander people?
7. You're really smart for one of them.
8. Aren't Aborigines and Torres Strait Islanders the same?
9. The situation with Aboriginal people is really an Aboriginal problem.
10. How are you a real Aborigine if you live in the suburbs?
11. I worked with one once and they were alright except when they had to go to a funeral and went walkabout for a week.
12. What percentage of you is Aboriginal? Are you half-caste or quarter-caste?

REMEMBER!

We have all been brainwashed into believing the SNL, that is why it has been so effective as a history shaper.

Short-Term Impacts on Indigenous Professionalism and Leadership

Aboriginal and Torres Strait Islander professionals and leaders are under constant tension and pressure in having to:

1, Diplomatically and powerfully manage themselves around people's ignorance and scepticism of their identity, their position, their credentials and their authority.
2. Stay true to their Blackfulla cultural principles whilst navigating the Whitefella world.
3. Continually give cross-cultural and history lessons to their Whitefella staff or colleagues.
4. Put themselves in the firing line of Blackfulla politics and community divisions.
5. Constantly deal with lateral violence and the threat of being called a big noter or being criticised and ostracised if the Black community think you are moving ahead and/or speaking on their behalf.
6. Be publicly accountable to do your job well, make a difference and get results. To do this, many Blackfullas become super high achievers to the point of being workaholics, often resulting in them over-committing themselves, often leading to some form of identity conflict, family or relationship breakdown or they suffer from a lifestyle or stress related health condition often requiring medication.

Long-Term Impacts on Indigenous Professionalism and Leadership

SNL Is In Your Body...

There is enough evidence to prove the SNL brainwashing campaign has worked and is indeed still at work. From a new science perspective, there is an evil genius in the deceptiveness of the SNL that we don't think was ever really predicted.

Over time, the SNL has been wired into our brain, encoded into our hearts and lives within the cells of our body. When the SNL is activated it registers within our body as dangerous. Guess what? As you will learn in Chapter 6, *"What Everybody Ought To Know about Running Your Own Brain,"* your brain does not like bad stress or threats of any kind, it literally gets freaked out.

Your body's equilibrium becomes unbalanced, triggering the body's natural stress reaction known as the fight, flight or freeze response. As a result, your brain signals the body to do whatever it takes to survive the perceived threat and get your body back into balance as soon as possible. This is an automatic, inbuilt survival mechanism.

Here is the Bad News Insight...

The SNL *'Blackfullas aren't as good as Whitefellas'* has literally been physically wired into our brain and encoded into our body. Your body has registered the SNL as a threat. We have internalised the lie at a psychological level, a spiritual level and a physical level. That is why the impacts of the SNL occur as so evasive and elusive. You can't always see the immediate impacts and you may not even be able to always name them, but your heart and body can always feel them.

When we try and make changes or if we get stressed or threatened by a statement like, *"all you Blackfullas are the same ...!"* this is enough to prepare our brain for battle. We then automatically do whatever it takes to survive the battle, just like our ancestors did during invasion. Our automatic reactions can range from punching the person in the mouth, to leaving the room quickly and then privately breaking down in tears, to being frozen and unable to move or speak, wishing the ground would swallow you up.

Can You Handle a New Truth?

For some of us Blackfullas, our brains are wired so that every day is invasion day. This gives you a glimpse of how trauma gets trapped within our bodies holding us hostage and emotionally hijacking our ability to reason and heal from painful experiences.

We assert that the fight-flight-freeze response, which is our body's natural mechanism for keeping us safe and alive, has also served to keep us trapped within an inter-generational cycle of trauma, dysfunction and disadvantage (TDD).

The new sciences of neuroscience, epigenetics, energy cardiology and mind-body medicine, supports this assertion and over time this inter-generational cycle of TDD has become imprinted within our biology and our cultural psyche.

Our Blackfulla culture in the 21st century looks very different to the way it was in the 17th century. Invasion and colonisation happened and we and our cultures have had to change in order to live and grow.

We have had to adapt to our new environmental conditions of colonial dominance or the extermination project would have been a success. Today, even many of our very ancient and most sacred cultural practices and lores will have come under pressure in some way to be altered in order to survive this new world we live in.

We continue to live in two worlds and at times it can be hard going!

In the beginning we had no choice but to take on much of White Australia's ways and it was not fair, just or right.

I believe we have always known within our hearts and spirits that if Australia in return would embrace the richness of the offerings and wisdoms of its First Nations cultures and our in-love-ness and deep respect for the Land and our connectedness to all things, then Australia would rightly hold its title as *The Lucky Country*.

Contemplate this next statement and question very carefully.

As Aborigines and Torres Strait Islanders we have gone through many overwhelming changes, resulting from the effectiveness of the brainwashing campaign, *"Blackfullas aren't as good as Whitefellas."* What if, by default, the inter-generational cycle of TDD is cunningly becoming part of our 21st century collective Blackfulla cultural identity?

Think about it…!

Is it possible that this lie has been internalised as a deep seated belief and could be a significant contributing factor in why so many of our kids are continuing to struggle with learning and academic success in mainstream schools, why we are plagued by lifestyle and stress-related diseases, why mental health issues are on the increase, why we are dying so young, why our young ones are committing or attempting to commit suicide and why we have become sufferers of identity conflict and leadership exhaustion?

What THE…!

Now before you go getting all wild up about what we said, we encourage you to think outside the box you live in.

Look through the eyes of our youth who are living in states of hopelessness in remote communities because they are bombed up on petrol to kill the pain because they can't read, can't get a job, can't get a woman or are sick of being used by men.

Look into the eyes of their parents who are burying them because they've hung themselves or have killed their cousins while they were charged up.

Look into the eyes of our kids sitting in urban schools, staring out the window wishing their dad didn't have to go back to jail for flogging mum again.

Look through the eyes of our young mothers who are having their third child and aren't even 20 years old yet, who are trying to stop themselves smoking yarndi during their pregnancy but are still drinking grog because they are stressed out knowing this kid will probably go into care as well and that their man is sleeping with their cousin.

Look into the eyes of our kids who go to private schools and still get called a nigger and only feel valued when they are playing sports.

Look into the eyes of our grandparents who are caring for their grandkids because….

If this is not enough, then ask our younger generation what it is like for them to be a Blackfulla in the 21st century; dig a little deeper and see what you find. Really listen to how all the good stuff about our cultural expression has been mixed up with all the negative stereotypes and have contributed to them forming their identity.

If this is still not enough to convince you, then read the latest national reports on Indigenous disadvantage and ask *why are we still getting these results in 2014?*

> There is much work to be done, but we can't transform what we don't acknowledge. It is vital that we begin having the hard uncomfortable conversations with each other, whilst keeping our vision for a proper deadly future in existence.

When our healing and transformation is being led by us Fullas and empowered with support from others, STARS Institute strongly believes we can go from surviving to thriving, and that the first step starts with you!

We've got to work on ourselves whist we are working with our Mobs or nothing will ever be sustainable. We are the space in which possibilities for others exist and this is a very sacred position.

The self-care cultural education practices we are about to introduce you to are simple things you can use immediately to begin the inner cultural and personal healing work that is needed and required.

If you think the practices are too simple, that is because they are. You will recognise that some of these practices have been used in the areas of health, well-being, juvenile justice and education...

STARS Institute recognises that these practices are central to cultural sustainability.

It's Weird But It Works

Short-Term Simple Strategies with a Long-Term Profound Impact

Self–Care Cultural Education Practices

This self-care cultural education is designed to begin decolonising your thinking and eliminating the invisible hold the SNL has on your identity. Part of this very sacred process is challenging and shifting our current perceptions and paradigms of who we are as First Nations peoples.

It will begin to ground your cultural identity and reconnect you back to the sacredness of who you are, as belonging to the longest living culture in the world.

As you make self-care cultural practices part of **your lifestyle**, a natural process of spiritual and heart healing will begin and you may notice internal shifts start to happen as your ancient cultural codes of wisdom begin to unlock from your DNA.

You may even notice your general health and well-being become re-energised and you experience a boost in your cultural esteem and self-expression.

The self-care cultural educational practices empower you to begin decolonising and liberating your own thinking, intellect and spirit from the shackles of colonial conditioning and the brainwashing of the SNL.

Build Cultural Well-Being and Capital

Our identity and spirituality as an Aborigine or Torres Strait Islander is our greatest strength as leaders. Our culture is the strongest foundation to our success and to the success we desire for others.

LEADERSHIP PRINCIPLE

Stop buying into the myth that our culture has died altogether and our identity is lost. It has not. Remember we are intelligent, resilient and resourceful! It is our responsibility to rediscover our culture, renew it, respect it and define our identity!

1. **Continue to develop a sacred relationship and respect for *your* country, *your* ancestral bloodlines, and *your* stories.**
   a. Spend time on *your* traditional country with your mob as often as you can. Walk Country in bare feet and in silence so that you can feel and watch Her talking to you. Our modern lifestyles have numbed our bodies from listening to the sacred teachings of our land and feeling the heart-stories of our Country.
   b. If you can't get to *your* country or you are unsure of where it is, that's okay. Find a special place in nature where you feel safe and at peace; where you feel you have a sense of connection and belonging. Spend time there often.
   c. Carry a picture of a special place from your Country and when you can't get there look at the picture or think about Country in a good way until you feel a sense of connection and inner peace.
   d. Where possible, learn the traditional and contemporary stories of your ancestral estate.

e. Talk to your ancestors often. If you're not sure how, start with acknowledging them and thanking them for continuing to be in your life and for the guidance they provide. Ask them questions and then be patient and wait for an answer. It might not always come in the way you expect it. Watch for their messages through nature. I have kookaburras visit me and tap on my windows each time I am deep in contemplation and moving through healing and creation cycles. It is excitement all round at my house when Kabul the carpet snake, which is my totem, comes for a visit. My sons, Lawson and Archie, and I feel a sense of being cared for and protected.

f. Hunt, gather and eat your traditional bush tucker as often as you can. No matter if you have got to prepare it in a microwave – get it into ya! Eating your traditional foods builds your wellbeing and health and strengthens your spiritual connection and oneness with your country and your mob.

g. Start your family tree if you don't already have one or start collecting your family stories and histories, especially the powerful and positive ones that will sustain you in challenging times.

h. Learn the name of the Country you currently live on and who the traditional owners are. Make it a habit of acknowledging their Ancestors.

i. Where possible, learn your language. Even if it is only a few words. Build these words into your vocabulary and use them often. Notice how your cultural confidence grows and it makes your body feel good when you speak your language.

2. **Empower your identity by knowing your black history.**

a. Talk to Elders and listen to their stories, they are our spiritual gatekeepers for grooming and esteeming our cultural identity. Learn through their stories to distinguish the many leadership messages and principles for life. Retraining our modern ears to listen for the cultural wisdoms that are within the stories of our Elders is an art we must learn to master again. This is called deep listening or, as we call it at STARS Institute, 'listening for the gold.'

    b. Continue to educate yourself on Blackfulla history and current affairs. Create time to do this. It could be as simple as spending 20 to 30 minutes a week reading, thinking, on YouTube, talking, blogging, on Facebook or journaling.

    c. You don't have to know everything but as a leader in the 21st century it is important that you do develop a political muscle and have informed thinking and positions about the current issues. Where possible, contribute *positively* to debates, conversations, protests or marches.

    d. Seek out historical trailblazers, read, Google and YouTube them. Many of these legends, which include communities, are masterful strategists.

    e. Become familiar with the United Nations Declaration on the Rights of Indigenous Peoples and use it as a living document to empower the work you do.

    f. Keep up to date and actively contribute to the latest issues impacting Blackfullas which include constitutional recognition, latest developments with the Closing The Gap strategy, the Stronger Futures in the Northern Territory Act and proposed changes to the Racial Discrimination Act.

    g. Become familiar with non-Indigenous people who have been supporters of, and advocates for, the right of our First Nations peoples, such as Faith Bandler, Fred Hollows, Gordon Bryant, Stan Davey, Don Dunstan, Jessie Street, HC "Nugget" Coombs, Jack and Jean Horner, Fred Chaney, Ray Martin and Jeff McMullen.

3. **Affirm your Identity by hanging out with other positive Deadly Blackfullas who think like you and build strong empowering relationships.**

    a. You will know whether relationships are empowering by how you feel – whether you feel energised by them, or whether you feel heavy, flat and drained by them.

    b. Create your own leadership bank of Blackfulla role models and study them. Include elders, family leaders, local community leaders, national leaders in their areas of expertise, for example Lowitja O'Donoghue, Mick Dodson, Linda Burney, Nova Peris, Charlie Perkins, Chris Sarra, Pat O'Shane, Stephen Page, Cathy Freeman, Koiki Mabo, Gary Foley, Waverley Stanley, Warren Mundine, Gracelyn Smallwood, Patrick Dodson, Jackie Huggins, Jessica Mauboy, Neville Bonner, Noel Pearson, Steve Mam, Joseph Elu, Larissa Behrendt, Brian Butler, Kevin Gilbert, Michael Mansell, Tania Major, Jason Glanville, Leah Armstrong, Tanya Hosch, Terri Janke, Sandra Georgiou, Suzanne Thompson and Anita Heiss – among many others. Also world leaders like Oprah Winfrey, Nelson Mandela, Barack Obama, Martin Luther King, Malcolm X and Colin Powell.

c. Commit to finishing reading this book. Take notes in it, highlight the magic moments for yourself, dog-ear the pages, make comments and share concerns and complaints on our Facebook page, phone us and have a chat about what you've read......but finish reading it.

4. **Define your cultural identity. Get excited and design a mind map with empowering words, pictures, colours and diagrams etc to begin tapping into your subconscious and exploring who you are. The most important thing to remember whilst doing this is to have fun and get into your creative zone. Your brain loves this kind of inspired activity, it begins laying the neural foundations to support new paradigm shifts. Take your time with this, there are no right or wrong ways to do it...just do it! Answer the following questions.**

a. What does your culture mean to you?

b. What do you love about your culture?

c. What elements of your culture give you the most strength and why?

d. How have these strengths shaped your cultural identity?

e. If you could consciously incorporate these strengths into your leader's identity and practices, how would you do it?

5. **Design a physical expression (painting, drawing, song, sculpture...) of your own modern day creation/dreaming story which captures your identity, values, beliefs and philosophies and connects you back to *your* country, *your* mob. Let your creative juices flow.**

   a. Place this object somewhere you will see it often. This will powerfully anchor your identity and connection back to your country and *ya* mob.

6. **Protect your identity.**

   a. Prepare yourself for racism and discrimination (R&D) but don't expect it. Feeling self-confident about your ability to manage and appropriately respond to R&D reinforces your positive self-image, self-acceptance and identity and builds psychological resilience. Check out the great video called, "*How To Tell People They Sound Racist*" on the Creative Spirits website www.CreativeSpirits.info in the section, *How to Deal With Racist People.*

   b. Develop a no-tolerance attitude towards lateral violence. It does not work for the future of our children to be running each other down. It is hoped that this book will empower you to be strong, positive and expressive in your identity and that you in turn will empower others to be the same.

   c. Remove the word "*Shame*" from your speaking...even when you are being funny. There is no place for it.

> When you belong you are strong.
> When you believe you achieve!
>
> **Wendy Watego**

Build Your Leadership Capacity

1. Define what YOUR leadership means to you? This is a starting point.
2. Seek out for yourself an Aboriginal or Torres Strait Islander mentor/s who is in a higher position or who has had more experience than you (this includes the wisdom and life experiences of Elders). Look for someone who has got the kind of results you want to accomplish or who can empower you to successfully navigate your way around the workplace and Blackfulla politics.
3. Seek out a coach who can work with you to;
    a. Develop a life or career plan
    b. Keep you accountable to fulfilling your vision and plan
    c. Support you when you hit a wall
    d. Teach you strategies for overcoming challenges
4. Become a life-long learner of leadership and make it a lifestyle. Look for Indigenous specific and mainstream training and education opportunities to support you mastering the craft of leadership.
5. Make a list of all your leadership strengths, gift and talents. Concentrate on consistently improving each of your strengths by just 1%. Enjoy the magic that unfolds as you begin working from your strengths.
6. Become an avid reader/researcher. Leaders are readers. Ensure you include reading books by Aboriginal and Torres Strait Islander authors.
7. Three 'muscles' that you must build continually in order to be a self-sustainable and highly effective leader:
    a. Your capacity to communicate with intention and impact;
    b. Your emotional intelligence; and
    c. Your ability to create and sustain an empowering mindset.

What we love about the Self-Care Cultural Education practices and the other strategies within this book is that we get to be the drivers of the bus and not a passenger at the very back of the bus. We are 100% responsible for liberating ourselves from the trap of the SNL. Only then can we empower others to do the same.

It starts with us taking charge of defining who we are and what we stand for and then being willing to be accountable for the choices we make and the life we lead.

If you are waiting for the SNL, racial stereotypes and baseless assumptions or ignorance to disappear before you declare yourself as liberated, you could be waiting a while.

> Grounding yourself in a strong identity can be the difference between dreaming, believing and achieving – and drifting, complaining and failing.

Section 2 of *'Out Of The Box Thinking on Indigenous Leadership'* has been designed to be quite distinct from this first section. Be warned, it may seem bizarre that the next section has you examining yourself from the inside out.

You might even think this book is insane and a load of BS and you would be right. It IS a load of BS – your Belief Systems! Some are old and outdated and some are ugly – and they are keeping you trapped and making you sick.

Allow me to share my definition of insanity with you…knowing you have been brainwashed to believe you are not as good as other people because you're Black and not being prepared to transform that mentality!

So strap yourself in, put a smile on ya dial and enjoy your journey!

SECTION TWO

> " This leadership program is different because it has given me the training I need to take control over my thoughts – a new skill that as a leader I have found has added such a valuable level to the way I approach and organise my life. "

STARS Program Graduate **Phyllis Marsh**
Student Services Manager

CHAPTER 5

The Secret of Your Leadership Blueprint™

What you need to know first and foremost is that there is an **inner world of leadership** and an **outer world of leadership** and although they are two different worlds, they are intimately connected and continually influencing each other.

The outer world of leadership includes how you express your leadership, apply leadership knowledge, manage people and take action. These are essential but the inner game is just as important. An analogy would be a surgeon and his/her operating equipment. Having the best operating equipment is imperative to the operation but being the best surgeon who can masterfully use the equipment and lead the surgical team is even more critical to the success of the operation.

People spend a lot of time, energy and money, in up-skilling and developing their outer world of leadership – which is of tremendous value. Imagine the quality of results which would be possible if you also invested your focus and attention on doing the inner work.

> **Consider that the outer work of transformation cannot be sustained until the inner work is done!**

If you are happy with the quality of your leadership at the moment, that is awesome. You will find that a lot of what we will be sharing in Section 2 of the book will resonate with you and affirm who you are and what you are doing.

But if you are not happy with your leadership at the moment, we invite you to consider some new possibilities that may not fit into your 'box' of what you currently think is the right and appropriate way of being a good leader.

We recommend you try out what we suggest. **Test it on yourself** and you will then know for sure what works and what doesn't.

What if you already had a model which was perfect for you and already existed within you? Our approach is not about imposing a Blackfulla leadership model or framework upon you. Instead, it is like that of Michelangelo the artist when he sculpted the statue David from marble; you get to chip away at everything that is not you – until the real leader appears.

There are going to be some of you who disagree with what we say and protest that it doesn't fit into the arena of leadership. Yes, perhaps you are right. Considering how the SNL has programmed our thinking and contributed to forming our beliefs about leadership, you have every right to be suspicious and sceptical.

But everything we talk about here does apply to your life. Consider that who you are and how you do life, is who you are and how you do leadership.

We are going to invite you to trust the ideas you are reading, apply them, play with them and let us know if they worked or didn't work for you. What we do know to be true is that they have worked for us and for the people we have worked with over the last six years.

Breaking free from the chains of the SNL and the bondage of the past is ultimately your decision. If you want to change the direction of your life and move your leadership to a whole new level it is up to you. In order to do this you need to be willing to let go of some of your old ways of thinking and being and embrace new ones.

The results will eventually appear for themselves.

LEADERSHIP PRINCIPLE

If you want a different result then be prepared to think and do things differently!

Want to Know What a Leadership Blueprint is?

As an analogy, let's look at a blueprint for a building. It is a plan that has been specifically designed for the safe construction and completion of a building.

When a builder reads the blueprint, everything they need to know is in the plan. They know what needs to happen to turn it from a drawing on paper into a building on the ground.

Your leadership blueprint is very much like the blueprint for a building, it is simply your personal plan for who you *are* as a leader and how you operate.

Here Is Why It Is Vital That You Know What Your Leadership Blueprint Is!

In Chapter 4, *Announcing a New Era of Blackfulla Leadership,* you were introduced to Self-Care Cultural Education. This education is essential in beginning to decolonise our thinking by refocusing and acknowledging the sacredness of who we are as First Nations peoples, and building on the strengths of our culture and our identity as a foundation for who we are as leaders.

Up until now, for many of us, our mind space has been infiltrated by a deficit model of what it is to be a Blackfulla leader. This has often resulted in a lot of energy being spent in trying to correct the perceived deficiencies that others have imposed upon us. This has limited our self-awareness, thwarted our potential, stunted our relationship with ourselves as leaders and impacted the development of our leadership blueprint.

Maximising your full potential as leaders is possible but it requires an ongoing commitment to master your internal world.

We all know of Blackfulla leaders who appear to be doing a really good job and then all of a sudden bang, something happens and they're out of the game.

Have you noticed that you have been guilty of getting in the way of your own leadership success? Have you noticed that Blackfullas hit a cultural glass ceiling in leadership? Have you noticed that there are some people who are extraordinary as leaders in their areas of expertise but the rest of their life sucks?

On the outside we can justify why we didn't go for that job or we didn't want to be seen big-noting ourselves or why that leader failed or hit the glass ceiling, pointing fingers and making assumptions like it probably had something to do with discrimination and not being supported. Of course, given the craziness of attitudes, behaviours, policies and procedures which smell of discrimination, racism and ignorance this could be the case.

But nonetheless, we enable it by allowing it to stop us in our tracks.

On the inside, however, something else is going on. Have you noticed that it feels like you are constantly trying to play catch up and you're not even sure how you got behind? That's why, if you or your community create, or are presented with, a huge opportunity which requires strong leadership and you're not ready for it on the inside, the chances are that your success will be short-lived.

This Is How Your Leadership Blueprint Got Developed

The foundation of your leadership blueprint started to develop during your younger years and is built upon as you grow. You are not even aware that many of your life experiences go towards shaping your blueprint.

Your leadership blueprint consists largely of **information** from your **past** that you have been specifically **taught** or automatically **programmed** with. Yes, this includes being brainwashed to believe the SNL.

Usually the information is determined by your life **experiences** and what you **make** those experiences mean.

....

EXAMPLE

*When I was growing up it was my Dad who was the major decision maker in my family and Mum was like a silent partner. I grew up **thinking** and **believing** that only men were the authority figures and only they could be the leaders of families. What men said ruled, no questions asked. If you didn't like it, too bad so sad.*

*I often **thought** that this 'man ruled belief' was unfair and as I grew into a woman I began to **feel** a silent fear, anger and resentment towards all men in authority, thinking they were all trying to tell me what to do.*

To the outside world I appeared to be a woman who was strong, resilient, self-reliant and capable, however, my identity as a leader was weak. My effectiveness as a key player in Indigenous education was being impacted. When working with men I would appear confident and supportive of decisions made by them. Even if I didn't agree, I would rarely speak up or share my ideas, views and opinions.

On the inside I began to feel myself becoming dependent on men to do my thinking and deciding for me and then resenting them for it. There were times when I felt like I'd never grown up and I had to do what I was told. This really sucked! I was secretly giving the middle finger to any man who tried to assert any authority over me – in a very professional way of course!

I finally thought, if I can't beat 'em I'll join 'em. As a result I grew a set of balls and literally began leading in schools like a man. I completely lost my femininity and my capacity to connect with any woman who I considered was too 'girly'.

What Did I Make All This Mean About Me and Leadership?

1. Only men were leaders.
2. As a leader it was your job to tell people what to do.
3. People should do what the leader tells them.
4. There is always a way to undermine the leadership of people you feel threatened by.
5. I don't trust myself to make decisions.
6. I don't value my own intuition and judgment.

Needless to say, my beliefs and approach to leadership was not going to support the huge vision I had. I was *Ms Dysfunction in heels and a suit* and I had about as much self-awareness as a nit.

LEADERSHIP PRINCIPLE

Self-awareness empowers you to be able to freely navigate your inner world and better predict and manage the results in your outer world.

Quick...This is Who Influenced Your LBP

The development of your leadership blueprint is strongly influenced by your relationships and life experiences.

This includes relationships with your parents, caregivers, grandparents, elders, sisters, brothers, cuzzies, teachers, enemies, sports coaches, friends and authority figures… Experiences include things that happen within your culture, community, school, media, technology, religion, dormitories, churches and the workplace.

Have a think about other significant people or events in your life that you can now see had a big impact on you. Chances are that they too played a part in helping you develop your blueprint for leadership.

Find Out What Your LBP is Made Up Of

There are many components which all work in unison and simultaneously to make up your leadership blueprint. These include: beliefs, culture, vision, values, philosophies, identity, habits, language patterns, behaviours, thoughts, emotions, plans, relationships and specialist knowledge and skill sets.

In this book the three core elements we are going to focus on, which encompass all the components of your LBP are: your thoughts, your emotions and your actions.

These three core elements always work together at the same time and they will **always** produce a specific result. We call this the T.E.A. equation:

Thoughts + Emotions + Action = RESULT

What you **think** causes you to experience a certain **emotion** and that emotion causes you to take certain **action** and that action causes a specific **result**.

Hurry…Your LBP is Hiding Here

Unlike the plans for a building which are easily accessible because they are usually centrally located, your leadership blueprint is stored deep within your subconscious mind. It literally lives within your inner world.

Your subconscious mind is a very powerful communications and information processing centre – it operates 24/7 and is responsible for 90% of your mind power. The remaining 10% is the job of your conscious mind.

Imagine if you were to walk into a big, high security warehouse full of storage shelves. On the shelves were filing drawers filled with information, data and memories about you from the moment of conception. Every piece of information is registered, cross-referenced and then archived. Your subconscious warehouse contains files from your past and these files govern who you are and how you live your life right now!

If you were to open up a file which read FRIENDS it will be referenced to every friend you have, have had or want to have. It will include references to all the memories, feelings, beliefs and thoughts about these friends and friendships in general. Possibly it could link you to the file on DECEPTION because you have a memory of a story your father repeatedly told you about a friend of his who stole the neighbour's milk money and then blamed him for it. It could also then link you to a file on TRUST and in this file you have a belief that says, "*your friends can't be trusted.*"

The simple file called FRIENDS could potentially be linked to 100,000 other files which could be located in 100,000 different places in the warehouse.

As a result of this file you may find that you don't have what you would consider to be many really close friends. You could even find it hard to trust the friends you do have.

You see, up until this point it was highly unlikely that in your subconscious warehouse you had a centrally located file that was specifically called "LEADERSHIP BLUEPRINT".

Your current blueprint for leadership is made up of lots of information from your past which is filed all over the place. Some of your files might be called LEADERSHIP file, BIG NOTER file, EMPOWERMENT file, BEING FIRED file, PARENTING file, REVENGE file…you get the picture?

Discover What Your Current LBP Is

Your leadership blueprint is located in lots of different files in your subconscious warehouse. To begin bringing your leadership blueprint to the surface of your consciousness, please take 2 minutes to do the questionnaire below. Work through the questionnaire quickly; if you mull over the statements for too long your conscious mind takes over and starts to analyse the questions and then your answers won't be a true reflection of your leadership blueprint.

Leadership Blueprint Questionnaire

Rate yourself on the following statements. (1) Being not true at all, to (5) being very true.

Success attracts success

Being a successful leader is a struggle and hard work most of the time

I am good at coping with pressure and stress

I feel pressure from White people to be an expert on all things Indigenous

To become a successful leader I will have to give up my personal life

I have a strong work ethic and I know my values

☐ No one takes me seriously because I am a Blackfulla with white skin

☐ If I become too successful, people will try and bring me down

☐ I have experienced racism in my workplace

☐ My parents were great parents, they always did the best they could

☐ I didn't have a good childhood, there is no way I can be successful

☐ I'm having to give cross-cultural lessons to my White colleagues so that they recognise, understand and respect my Blackfulla world view

☐ I can still take intelligent action in spite of feeling fearful, worried or upset

☐ I plan for success, either for myself or others

☐ I am proud of our Blackfulla history, in spite of all that's happened we have a story of resilience, ingenuity and survival to be proud of

☐ I'm in a healthy relationship and I have my partner's support

☐ I know I believe in some of the stereotypes about my Mob

☐ I achieve my goals or visions at least 70% of the time

☐ Successful people are arrogant and can't be trusted

- [ ] My parents were positive role models of what it means to be good leader

- [ ] Deep down inside I don't trust White people

- [ ] I am in good health and I have a positive sense of wellbeing

- [ ] My life will change for the better when I become a better leader

- [ ] Being scared and still being able to take action is a strong character of leadership

- [ ] I have felt excluded in life because I'm a Blackfulla

- [ ] It's not part of my culture to be seen to be a successful leader

- [ ] I don't feel I'm good enough to be a leader

- [ ] If I become successful it will stop people from liking me

- [ ] I have stuff in my past which stops me from being a leader

- [ ] Asking people for help is a sign of weakness

- [ ] My leadership is not impacted by inter-generational trauma and history

- [ ] Having goals is important

- [ ] It's very important to me to have time for myself

☐ I have a very big vision for my life and where I want to go and I know I can do it

☐ Leadership means giving up my culture

☐ I hate it when other people go big-noting themselves

☐ I worry about what other people think of me

☐ I want to make a difference in the lives of my family and community

☐ Getting a good education or job is important

☐ I know who I am, what I am capable of and where I want to go

Now, review your answers and highlight each statement which you feel has been impacted by the SNL, racism or inter-generational trauma.

Notice how you approached this whole task! Was it with enthusiasm or did you skip over it and complain that there were too many questions, that they were too ambiguous or that the SNL doesn't apply to you?

The attitude you had when you did this questionnaire begins to distinguish your leadership character, your commitment to results, your willingness to allow others to contribute to you and your leadership sustainability.

It highlights your current relationship to the outer world of leadership and the value you place on your own self-development. Having you rate yourself for the questions gives you immediate access into your inner world of leadership, providing you with an awareness about how you are currently wired to experience and express leadership.

TASK

On reflection of your responses, answer the following questions and just notice what comes up for you.

1. What did you learn most about yourself?

_____

_____

_____

_____

2. Did any of your ratings surprise you and why?

_____

_____

_____

_____

3. What did you just realise about the SNL?

_____

_____

_____

_____

4. How has your leadership been influenced by inter-generational grief and trauma?

_____

_____

_____

_____

Do You Know Who Really Owns Your Leadership Blueprint?

Have you noticed that your leadership blueprint is a plan which has been designed FOR you, but not BY you?

It is a plan for leadership that lives within you but has been hidden from you. It is based on the impacts of grief and trauma and outdated information from past experiences and relationships.

It seems incredibly strange to even ask this question but here goes......

Whose leadership blueprint is it?

That's right…it's not yours! It belongs to all those people of influence from your past. It has been passed on to you directly and indirectly by generations of people who had it passed down to them. You have been trying to lead successfully and navigate life in the modern world with an old plan for leadership from the past that's not even yours.

No wonder the blueprint has been hard to read!

What you are now becoming conscious of is all the unfinished business that you inherited from the past which is putting a lid on what you are really capable of. If you choose to take no notice of the reality that you have unfinished business, then it is like ignoring a small crack in a big dam wall. Eventually the pressure is going to build up and it will bust wide open.

As you work through the book and identify other areas of your leadership blueprint you'll find an appreciation starts to develop for how much power you actually have in recreating and controlling your life.

LEADERSHIP PRINCIPLE

As you expand your awareness of your leadership blueprint you expand your awareness for your life!

Discover How To Start Creating A New Leadership Blueprint

It's Weird But It Works

Right now you have the opportunity to begin consciously creating **your** very own new leadership blueprint.

Now as wombi as the process may sound, it is important that you follow the instructions, have a laugh and play full out.

If you commit to doing this rather odd yet simple task, chances are you will instantly experience a shift in the way you feel about yourself. I love this process because it begins to shake you up and interrupt your habitual patterns of 'judgmental thinking and negative self-talk' which automatically kicks in whenever you feel uncomfortable.

Are you ready? Here goes.

1. Stand up. Remember a time when you achieved something that made you feel real deadly and proud. Now stand the way you stand when you feel successful, deadly and real proud... good job!

2. While you're feeling this way squeeze your dominant hand and say "*YES!*" Notice that when you are standing like this and said the word YES there was a confidence in your voice... good job! Do it until your body feels it.

3. Say out loud, using the same confident voice you said YES with, "*I am creating my new leadership blueprint now!*" and then again squeeze your most dominant hand and say "YES!" Continue to repeat this step until you're feeling proper Deadly.

4. OPTIONAL BUT VITAL – if you're serious about creating a new leadership blueprint and embedding it into your inner world. Then it is just as important that you do things which are practical to bring it to life in your outer world as well.

   a. Get yourself a leadership journal/notebook/file.

   b. In your most creative handwriting write on the journal, *My Leadership Blueprint*.

c. Once you have done this, hold your journal and while looking at it say out loud, using your voice of success and confidence, "*My leadership blueprint,* YES!"

d. You will be filling this file with some cool and fun stuff as you read and work your way through the book so keep it on standby each time you are reading.

Sounds weird doesn't it? Trust us, this simple task has just given you security clearance to all records in your subconscious warehouse. You will now be able to locate any files your conscious mind requires, yes even your X-files so that you can use them to continue creating your **new** leadership blueprint.

So now, if you are ready to lead and live a life you love, freed up from the constraints of your past, we need to hook you up to someone who is going to be vital to your leadership journey.

Please meet your newest best friend – your brain.

" Biology gives you a brain.
Life turns it into a Mind.

Jeffrey Eugenides

CHAPTER 6

What Everybody Should Know About Running Their Own Brain

Hi, I'm your brain talking directly to you. Yes, I'm your new best friend. You and I have never formally been introduced even though we've been hanging out together for years. I will probably know more about you than you will ever know about me but don't panic my big eyed friend, even modern science hasn't built a machine that comes close to matching the intelligence of who I am and what I can do.

I have got to tell you that I am excited about working with you in a conscious way because together we can change your life and your leadership into a brand new level of awesome-ness…

Why it is Important To Run Your Own Brain

REMEMBER!

If your thinking is stinking, then your results are too!
Leadership is as much an inside job as it is an outside job!

We all agree that the historical legacy of the SNL and the Black history of Australia have shaped our collective perceptions and experiences of life! Many of us have even dedicated our lives to correcting these injustices through the work we do.

Thankfully we are now at a time in history where Black Australia is awakening and beginning to reject the imposed paradigms of discrimination, dysfunction and disadvantage. We are beginning to take back leadership in defining who we are and what we are capable of. We're reconnecting with our Ancestors and returning to the wisdoms that come from knowing we are the peoples from the longest surviving culture on the planet. We are now forging new paradigms of Blackness which value a strong identity, cultural renaissance, personal excellence, spiritual renewal and visions for the future to be enjoyed by all Australians.

STARS Institute is optimistic that our body of work will contribute to this new paradigm and with it usher in the new era of Blackfulla leadership. It is a call to action to individuals and communities to be vigilant about the old paradigms and beliefs of Blackness as they still dominate our experiences with messages of White superiority.

What's This Got To Do With The Brain?

Everything! What if our national brain is wired to accept that White people, particularly White privileged men, are the most valued people in our society? We can intellectualise and reject this message all we like but it doesn't weaken the collective authority of Australia's subconscious to hold the perception as being a truism.

Look at who dominates the public images around us.

Please understand that as a consequence of dormant dominant beliefs such as this, our national brain has laid down the neurological wiring for these perceptions of White superiority to propagate within us, whilst energising the brainwashing propaganda that *"Blackfullas aren't as good as Whitefellas."*

Certainly us Fullas have the aspirations, the intelligence and the potential to lead in a new social movement but our potency is compromised if, collectively, our cultural brain is wired to keep us believing that we are inferior. Unhealthy thinking like this harms any great intentions and any results we do get are not always sustainable.

Simple Yet Insightful...

The specialist education that STARS Institute has designed for *Running Your Brain and Mastering Your Biology* is extensive. What we have included in this chapter is a snapshot of why it is important to learn this knowledge and master these skills. You will get to understand how your thoughts (beliefs, perceptions, self-talk) plus emotions plus actions work together to *always* produce a result. We introduced this to you in Chapter 5, *The Secret of Your Leadership Blueprint* as the T + E + A equation.

Included in this chapter are loads of simple, fun and unorthodox ways in which you can train your own brain.

Some of what we suggest may seem weird but it works. Test it out on yourself *for at least a month* so you have an opportunity to measure your results. At the very least you'll have a laugh at yourself that will make you feel good and, in turn, boost your immune system.

Just by reading this book, parts of your brain have been sent into a quandary. The SNL does not like being brought out from its hiding place into the light of consciousness. As you will understand, it would prefer that things do not change and our brains have been conspiring with the lie right under our noses.

Want To Know A Little Secret?

This book truly is a living resource. Every word is designed to challenge your current paradigm of who you are as a Blackfulla and as a leader. Every word is designed to drive the SNL up and out of your mind, body and spirit. Every page is intended to decolonise your psyche, heal the legacy of inter-generational wounding and breathe a new life-force back into you.

Now, let's get started with some 'need to know' stuff on how our brain works!

Scientific Breakthrough – The Brain Can Change Itself

You have heard the saying, *"You can't teach an old dog new tricks."* It was once believed that by the time you were an adult your brain was hardwired for life and it and you could not be changed. It was a belief that had us thinking we were powerless to improve or change our lives and the circumstances we lived in. This thinking still exists and it puts a lid on human potential.

MYTH!!

New research by Dr Norman Doidge (2008) on neuroplasticity shows that the brain is malleable and can change and adapt each time it has a new experience. Modern research has demonstrated that the brain continues to create new neural pathways and alter existing ones in order to adapt to new experiences, learn new information and create new memories.

Vicki and I are so excited about neuroplasticity and the scope of the new sciences in their application to healing from the impacts of inter-generational loss, grief and trauma. What we are about to share with you is just the tip of the iceberg of the work we do but if you commit to applying what we suggest, consistently for a minimum of one month, then we guarantee that you will have results you are happy with.

When we are responsible for ourselves then we hold the key to our own healing. Our work in the areas of neuroscience and psychoneuroim-munology hands you back the power to let go of the constraints of the past, control your life and determine your future.

Have You Heard That Your Brain Is In Love With Negativity?

Have you noticed that we are very good at learning from bad experiences and bad at learning from good experiences? The answer is rooted deep within our genetic makeup: it's a phenomenon that scientists call *the negativity bias*.

This negativity bias means our brains are designed to pay more atten-tion and react more intensely and quickly to negative perceptions and experiences than to positive ones because, originally, it increased our odds of survival. When our ancestors were out hunting and gathering, it was more important for their survival to react if they heard, felt or saw danger approaching.

So, over time our brains have become like a magnet for negativity.

Psychologist Rick Hanson (2013 National Institute for the Clinical Application of Behavioural Medicine Webinar Series) explains that negative experiences have a dedicated memory system for survival. It is like the Rolls Royce of memory systems. It contains survival information that you would need to remember if you had to learn how to escape a tiger, in case it happened again or if you had to learn how to deal with alcoholic parents and family violence, you would want to remember how to do that.

Positive experiences also have a dedicated memory system but it is not as powerful as the negative memory system…

LEADERSHIP PRINCIPLE

You have the power to consciously turn negative perceptions into positive expectations!

Our brains are very sensitive to negativity and if our thoughts are negative and left unchecked, our emotions will go wild – disrupting our heart energy and encouraging the negative thoughts to govern over the top of our positive ones.

Have you noticed when you are on a roll of negativity that it could last hours, days, weeks – yes, even years? Have you also noticed the moment you start having good things happen in your life your mind starts to anticipate that something will soon go wrong? Your little voice inside your head starts to say things like, "*It can't last forever, all good things come to an end, the bubble is going to burst sooner or later...see I told you so, ya big noter!*"

Did You Know Your Brain Freaks Out Easily?

Guess what the brain's main job is? That's right, the main job of your brain is to keep you safe and alive! It is an inbuilt *threat-o-metre*.

The conscious mind is more comfortable with change and it likes to set itself goals and make plans for achieving change. But your subconscious mind does not like change of any sort and it is your subconscious mind that makes 90% of your decisions. It is the big Kahuna and will override any decisions made by your conscious mind in the blink of an eye.

How many New Year's Eve resolutions have you made but not fulfilled?

Change scares the brain and pushes it out of its comfort zone. The role of the brain is to keep you just the way you are now – warts and all. It depends on sameness and certainty to keep it happy, even if it is causing you pain. No change will take place until you have consciously changed the way you think and feel and directed your subconscious mind to form a new habit.

We can't stress this enough so please listen up!
News Flash…Your Brain Gets Stressed Out By
The Big C Word!

In the current paradigm of what it means to be a Blackfulla in this country, what is it that we are always trying to do, fighting to do, standing for, advocating for…? It's the big C word.

We want CHANGE! Yes?

We want to change our lives, change the circumstances, change the results, change the statistics and change Australians. Change, Change,

Change. Usually to move away from something undesirable. Guess what completely horrifies the brain? CHANGE! Your brain does not like you to, or want you to, change!

The stress of change is unpleasant even when it is transient. A stressful situation – such as worrying about a looming work deadline or the thought of being called a big-noter because you want to share your ideas at the next staff meeting – can trigger a cascade of stress hormones that activates your body's natural automatic survival response known as the fight, flight or freeze response.

This is a really powerful system because if you are being chased by a tiger or if late at night you are walking alone along a dark street and you hear heavy footsteps coming up quickly behind you, you are going to rely on this survival response to call you into action quickly.

The downside, however, is that the brain cannot tell the difference between a real physically life-threatening circumstance – such as being chased by a tiger/another human being – and a psychologically threatening circumstance – such as experiencing racism or being caught in a traffic jam.

On a physiological level, your body reacts to psychological stress and threats in exactly the same way as it would to a life or death situation.

Danger! You've Been Hijacked By Your Brain

When we feel threatened it causes our brain to become hijacked or what is also known as an emotional hijack.

Goleman (1996 p. 13-14) explains that when this happens a warning bell goes off and the stress hormones of adrenaline and cortisol are released throughout the body. It is signalling to your body to get ready for battle. Your body starts to pump blood to your arms and legs in case you need to defend yourself or run and your muscles tense. Your ability to reason disappears, emotions are spewing out, your pupils dilate and look like saucers, your heart is beating so fast and you are breathing so heavily you think your chest will explode. You are focused 100% on the threat – real or imagined!

The "fight-ers" will be thinking, "*Come on baby, bring it on!*" They will be ready to fight physically or verbally and either way, won't back down.

The "flight-ers" will be thinking, "*How can I get out of here quickly?*" They will be scanning the room for the nearest exist or waiting for a pause in conversation so that they can get out quickly.

The "freeze-ers" will be thinking, "*Just leave me alone, leave me alone, leave me alone.*" They may not be able to move or speak, they are like a kangaroo in the headlights.

Whilst this is taking place, your brain is searching the X-files in your subconscious warehouse for information and reaction strategies on how to deal effectively with this category of threat. Your reaction strategies are wired into your nervous system and when you are experiencing an emotional hijack you are on autopilot.

If you've got lots of positive reaction strategies, such as stopping what you're doing and taking deep breaths, choosing an optimistic attitude or going for a walk in the sunshine, then chances are you will have workable relationships and good results.

LEADERSHIP PRINCIPLE

Know what your automatic response is to stress and develop healthy strategies for managing yourself!

Do Your Strategies Suck?

However, if you've got a file full of experiences with not-so-great results, then chances are you have got files full of ineffective, unhealthy and disempowering strategies.

Either way, you will automatically use whatever strategies you have the most knowledge of and experience in. For example, if you are a parent, in your parent file you may have a strategy called, *scream at the kids when they won't do what you want and answer you back.* Well, that is what you will do. It is probable that this is how you were parented.

Here is the rub. As a leader, what is your first reaction when your team resists doing what you want them to do and starts to question you? Now, you may not literally scream at your staff the way you do your children but notice.... you don't have to open your mouth to scream *"do what I say and do it now!"*

Your current strategies for dealing with emotional hijacks have become habitual and even if you know at a conscious level that they are not working for you as well as they could, you will automatically continue using them because subconsciously that is habitually all you know. Your subconscious warehouse is loaded with files that are years old, have never been updated and no longer serve you.

I know, as an adult, I used to still throw a tantrum whenever I was emotionally hijacked. I didn't kick and scream like a 2 year old. I just stomped, scowled and sulked like a 40-year old.

REMEMBER!

Even when we consciously know our habits drain us, we will continue to use them because that is what we have subconscious files for!

Our research has shown that given our history and the deceptiveness of the SNL it is not uncommon for us Blackfullas to be living in a constant state of an emotional hijack. The intensity just varies between individuals and communities.

Prolonged time spent within an emotional hijack can lead to:

1. Being trapped within patterns of unhealthy thinking, decision making and limited choices.
2. Losing a sense of self-responsibility and shifting blame onto other people or circumstances. This keeps us locked within a victim mentality.
3. A breakdown in our health and emotional wellbeing.

What is important is recognising when we are experiencing an emotional hijack. The moment you are aware it is happening you have the power to choose to interrupt it and support your body while it is returning to its natural state of homoeostasis or balance.

It's Weird But It Works

Here are three strategies which, if used regularly, will support you in building up your emotional fitness muscles, empower you to interrupt and control emotional hijacks and enhance your health and well-being.

The first two strategies we highly recommend are:

1. Taking up the practice of regular meditation.
2. Learning the Emotional Hijack Interrupt.

Both these practices can be found on our website **www.StarsLeader shipInstitute.com**. Go to the Resources tab, then click on the Health & Wellbeing tab. You can download PDFs about each of these practices.

The third strategy which we are going to detail here is a quick and easy-to-use one. To get the most value out of this strategy practice it, practice it, practice it! Once your body is familiar with the strategy you will be able to generate supportive emotions on demand, increase your zest for life and expand your relationships.

LEADERSHIP PRINCIPLE

Good Leaders Manage Their Emotions BUT Great Leaders Generate Them!

How To Improve Your Emotions In 5 Minutes

When managing our emotions, our main aim is to reach for a better feeling emotion.

Esther and Jerry Hicks (2004 p.114) call this 'moving up the emotional scale.' All emotions are energy and either give you energy or drain you of energy. Notice how your energy levels are when you feel on top of the world. Now think about a time when you were feeling really sad, how was your energy level then? If you are feeling good you have high feeling, fast moving energy. If you are feeling bad you have heavy, slow moving energy.

Imagine your emotional energy (EE) is like an emotional fuel tank. To see how much EE you have in your tank you have to look at your EE gauge. When your emotional tank is full you are operating from higher emotions such as happiness, optimism or love and this is when you get the most mileage. These emotions have you feeling the most connected to yourself, others and life, giving you an inner sense of belonging and security.

When your EE tank is running low it is a good indication that you are living from your lower emotions such as grief, anger, jealousy, guilt or blame. This is usually when you feel most disconnected from yourself, others and life and it paves the way for your most dysfunctional moments.

A scale or gauge of your emotions would look something like this:

1. Joy/Knowledge/Empowerment/Freedom/Love/Appreciation
2. Passion
3. Enthusiasm/Eagerness/Happiness
4. Positive Expectation/Belief
5. Optimism
6. Hopefulness
7. Contentment
8. Boredom
9. Pessimism
10. Frustration/Irritation/Impatience
11. Overwhelmed
12. Disappointment
13. Doubt
14. Worry
15. Blame
16. Discouragement
17. Anger
18. Revenge
19. Hatred/ Rage
20. Jealousy
21. Insecurity/ Guilt/ Unworthiness
22. Fear/Grief/Depression/Despair/Powerlessness

Since the same words are often used to mean different things and different words are often used to mean the same things, these word labels for your emotions are not absolutely accurate for every person who feels the emotions. Don't let these words confuse or distract you from the purpose of learning to use the emotional guidance scale (Esther and Jerry Hicks 2004 p.114).

The thing that matters most is that you are CONSCIOUSLY reaching for a feeling that is an improvement and makes you feel better.

When I first started to train myself and my family in this strategy it felt strange because I was not used to being **conscious** of what I was feeling. I had to learn to distinguish the difference between feeling angry and being worried. After practicing moving up and down the emotional scale, I got that these two feelings are actually very different for me. That is why we encourage you to practice trying on the emotions so that you know how they feel for you.

It is like building up your emotional muscles, the more you work them out the stronger you become. The stronger you become emotionally the smarter your thinking, and the smarter your thinking the stronger you become emotionally.

LEADERSHIP PRINCIPLE

Self-Awareness Gifts You The Power Of Choice!

Here is how you reach for that improved feeling....

Stand up and stand the way you would stand if you were feeling anger. Feel that fully in your body. Now reach for another emotion that is further up the emotional scale, such as the emotion of being worried; now feel that fully in your body. Move to another emotion – frustration, then to boredom, then to contentment, next is hopeful. Notice that each time you move your way up the emotional scale you are feeling a sense of inner relief. That is the intention. Continue to work your way up the emotional scale until you reach an emotion that you are happy with...

Good job! You are on your way to mastering your emotions.

The Secret To Easy Change Is To Stop Frightening Your Brain

This is a great little strategy for preparing your brain for change. It is called, "Starting with the End in Mind," and is a process we use every day without knowing we are using it.

Let me give you an example. Before Edison invented the light bulb he first had to see a clear picture in his mind of what he wanted. He had to bring it to life in his inner world before he could produce the result in his outer world.

Pictures are the language of the brain and if you can see change happening in your mind before it happens, it can calm the brain down when change does occur because the brain is already familiar with it. In the words of Albert Einstein, *"Imagination is more important than knowledge."*

When you are expecting change, use your imagination to do two things:

1. Think about a simple change you would like to accomplish within the next week. Visualise yourself achieving that change and become fully aware of what the positive results will look like once it has been achieved. Bring the results alive in your mind and feel what the positive results will feel like. Hear what the positive results will sound like. What would you be saying to yourself when the change has been successfully accomplished?

   When your body feels good, anchor this feeling with a YES anchor!

2. Visualise the change not being achieved and look for the wisdoms in failing. This spins the mind out because it is not programmed to look for the positives in a negative situation. It is programmed to seek out more negatives.

   By doing this, you are interrupting old habitual ways of thinking and feeling and consciously programming yourself to think in new empowering ways.

What To Do To Get Your Brain To Co-operate With You

You must rehearse both of these scenarios with purpose and passion at least six times a day and for at least 30 seconds. It will be more successful if you feel happy and positive at the start and at the end of each visualisation. Notice the feel-good chemicals being released into your body.

The great part is that once you have focused the brain's attention on what change you consciously want, it will co-operate with you and start to hunt out resources and opportunities to accomplish this positive result. The conscious mind loves to go after clearly defined visions and goals which juice you up and feed the subconscious mind's compulsion for safety.

The other great outcome is even if your efforts of change are not successful, the brain won't freak out or be as overwhelmed as it might usually.

You have successfully begun training the brain into the helpful habit of looking for the positive in hard core challenging situations and staying optimistic. The value of building healthy mind practices is that it opens up your capacity to think divergently when solving problems, supports you to think on your feet and make good decisions when under pressure, activates the law of attraction and inspires people to work with you towards a common vision.

LEADERSHIP PRINCIPLE

Without conscious action, you are unlikely to achieve the results you want.

Try it out for one week. Take on looking for the positive learnings in negative situations. See what happens and how you feel at the end of one week. What will power up this process is, each time negativity presents itself, say in an expectant tone, *"What is the good in this situation?"*

Asking great quality questions supports the brain as it grows and heightens your emotional intelligence.

Oh, if you want a bonus strategy for using the creative juices of your visualisation try the following suggestion. Your brain gets huge value out of having a plan of action it can follow. A plan keeps it paying attention and activates your automatic goal setting/seeking mechanism. The moment you take control of your mind and start planning, you generally feel calmer, more focused and more on track.

In your leadership blueprint journal jot down some actions you can take to reinforce the vision you just created. You may be surprised that once you change your thinking and take new action, results begin to show up quickly. Don't be surprised if you have some mind-blowing unexpected outcomes show up.

How Our Brain Gets Wired For Life!

There are many complex steps that occur in wiring the brain and they all happen at the speed of light.

To keep it simple, let's pretend that when you were 5 you and your parents lived with your Aunty because your parents couldn't find a house to rent. You heard your Dad yell at your Mum, "*Those White bastards think they are better than us – they won't rent to us 'cause we're Blackfullas.*" This event was significant because you'd never heard your parents fight before.

You felt confused and a little scared and you repeated a version of what you think your dad said, "White people are better than us Blackfullas." In this moment your brain got fired up and it fired off the beginning of a neural pathway called, "*Blackfullas aren't as good as Whitefellas.*"

As you grew up, you had lots of experiences to prove this belief was true and you fell into the habit of automatically thinking like this.

Each time you think SNL thoughts it strengthens this neural pathway in your brain. It also triggers off other thoughts associated with the SNL such as, *you can't trust White people and there's something wrong with being Black…* The thoughts can become quite obsessive and intrusive. Before you know, it you have a whole lot of similar thoughts and experiences connecting and hanging out together in your brain, called a 'neural net.'

FREE BONUS

To watch a quick and funny video on how your brain gets wired and your neural networks get developed, go to our website **www.StarsLeadershipInstitute.com** then click on our YouTube channel and watch the video, "*Cheese Cake, Carrot Cake Wired, But Not For Life*".

Find Out How YOUR Network Is Working

A neural net is just like a corporate networking function where you meet like-minded people, build relationships and do business deals. Only this is happening in your brain.

The neural 'network' grows larger and stronger as more new thoughts compete for membership and deals are going down between which thoughts stay and which thoughts go. It is a busy place up there in the brain and your neural pathways are constantly fighting for prime space and optimum positioning. Eventually the neural net is firmly established and becomes a mindset also known as a paradigm, world view or belief system.

The SNL takes up an executive position on the neural net, as the CEO.

Test it out for yourself by saying the SNL out loud. "*Blackfullas aren't as good as Whitefellas.*" Observe that even if you don't believe it, be aware of the other thoughts that are activated and associated with the SNL. Write these thoughts in your leadership blueprint journal.

What do you make those thoughts mean and how have those thoughts moulded your identity, informed your leadership and influenced your relationship with White people? Notice now how you are feeling. Each time you have any thoughts about the SNL you have an automatic emotional reaction to it.

Facts You Need To Know About Your Brain and Your Emotions

Dr Candace Pert (1997) a neuroscientist found that each emotion we experience signals the brain and the body to release chemicals into your body which are a match for your emotion. Very simply, happy cheerful thoughts equal happy feel-good chemicals.

If you feel angry when you think about the SNL, your body releases the stress hormones and sends you into the fight-flight-freeze response we just spoke about. Depending on how you react emotionally to the SNL will depend on what chemicals are released into your body and how strong the SNL is imprinted into your nervous system.

Research has shown that there is no distinction between thinking and feeling. Your thinking becomes your emotions and your emotions become your thinking (2013 National Institute for the Clinical Application of Behavioural Medicine Webinar Series).

As much as laugh lines become engraved into the face of happy people, repetitive negative thoughts and emotions also leave their marks on your brain. What would your life and health be like if you only chose to predominantly think thoughts which made you feel good and empowered you, even when the circumstances were depressing? How would this kind of thinking begin to pump wellbeing back into you, free you up from the chains of the SNL, improve your life and expand your leadership?

It's Weird But It Works

Here is a quick way to begin breaking up the SNL neural network and interrupt your habitual patterns of thinking about it.

Language, emotions and imagery are the triad of transformation when it comes to rewiring the brain.

Every time you come face to face with the SNL and you start to feel wild or disempowered in any way, think of the words to that song, "*I'm sexy and I know it.*" So put a smile on your dial and to the tune of that song, sing "*I'm proud and deadly and I know it.*" And if you want to create your own dance moves and add more lyrics to go with it, better still. Whatever it takes for you to feel good. Being in public is no excuse not to do it.

Just thinking about doing this in your mind will make you feel joyful if you're really getting into it. Go on, try it! You see, the more trauma and unresolved upsets we have experienced the more conscious repetitive exposure we need to "feel good and positive" experiences. We have to start training the trauma out of our brains and our body.

Notice that we said train the trauma out of your body, not the memory. You may always have the memories of ugly experiences but your power lies in the meaning you give to those experiences and the emotional memories which are attached to those experiences.

Programming My Own Brain for Failure…

When you try to change something that is not working for you, such as giving up smoking and getting healthy, have you noticed how much inner resistance comes with it and a fear of failure steps in?

The little voice inside your head starts to run the show and point out examples of where and how you have failed before. This stresses you out even more, so you have another ciggie thinking, 'that will shut the voice up,' but the voice goes on to paint a picture of doom and gloom about your future without the ciggies. It has you beginning to feel the pain you'll have to go through to stop smoking, lose weight and get off the heart meds.

While all this is at play, the threat of failure has triggered your brain to go into the fight-flight-freeze response and prevents you from making a clear and sensible decision. The story in your head is on autopilot and won't shut up – and eventually you feel rotten. Got to numb that pain..... So you have another ciggie, washed down with a soft drink, chips, hamburger and a family block of chocolate.

The absurdity is, to the brain, there is less pain and threat in staying a fat, sugar-addicted diabetic smoker, then there is in going through the perceived pain of getting healthy.

LEADERSHIP PRINCIPLE

Fearing Failure Is No Reason To Give Up!

Learn How To Fail And Succeed At The Same Time

Fear of failure is the killer of dreams being fulfilled and greatness not being realised. As kids, failure was part of the fun of life and learning. There was joy in failing. Just watch our babies as they are learning to walk. Have you noticed they embrace failure with an aliveness? And success soon follows.

If we don't fail, we don't grow. You have all heard the cliché, '*You learn from your mistakes.*' Sheehan & Pearse (2012 p.41) say a psychologist from the University of Exeter discovered that you learn a lot more when your predictions are incorrect than when they are correct.

Your brain reacts in just 0.1 of a second when it sees something that has caused you to make a mistake in the past. Unless you've tried and made a mistake, how can you build this early warning system? Instinct for the right decision seems to be a characteristic of successful people.... but they build this strength by making mistakes.

The challenge for us is that we have been brainwashed to believe that our Blackness is somehow a failure. This potentially determines how much joy we experience in our leadership and the quality of health and well-being we experience in life.

LEADERSHIP PRINCIPLE

Failure is not who you are.
It is a result which tells you that you are closer to success!

When Thomas Edison went to school, a teacher told him he was too stupid to learn anything. When he was in the process of inventing the light bulb a young reporter boldly asked him if he felt like a failure and if he thought he should just give up. Perplexed, Edison replied, *"Young man, why would I feel like a failure? And why would I ever give up? I now know definitively over 9,000 ways that an electric light bulb will not work. Success is almost in my grasp."*

And shortly after that, and more than 10,000 attempts, Edison invented the light bulb (YouTube Famous Failures).

It's Weird But It Works

Here are two of the fastest, funniest and most inspirational ways ever to develop a healthy relationship to failure. What I love about these strategies is that you learn how to be the master of making yourself feel good by switching on the "feel good" switch in your brain and body. When you feel good and your mood is happy you are flooding your body with endorphins (Bloom 2001) which are a key component of optimum health, wellbeing, consciousness and unlimited possibilities.

1. Watch YouTube videos on famous people who rejected the labels of failure imposed on them and in time allowed their brilliance to contribute to the world. Famous people like Oprah Winfrey, Walt Disney, Richard Branson, Michael Jordan, Dr Seuss and our very own Aussie inspiration, **Nick Vujicic**.

2. Go on a 30 day failure hunt and develop a 'have a go' attitude. Each day look for ways to fail at something. When you fail say, "*Yes I did it. I failed but I had a go, I'm too deadly!*" Say it in a voice tonality which is playful, joyful and proud. This takes the seriousness and anxiety out of the F word and begins to desensitise the brain to failure, strengthens your heart energy and trains your brain to remain relaxed around potential threats of failure.

Advice To Leaders Who Value Emotions

Here's the best part ever, when the brain is in a natural relaxed feel-good state and you're having fun, you build up your emotional resilience muscles, your capacity to learn accelerates, you become more resourceful and you look younger.

But wait, there's more.

Funnily enough, you start to feel newly connected with people and have a drive to want to help out or contribute. People like being around you because they feel good and just as importantly you like being with other people.

Goleman (1996 p.114) explains that when people catch each other's moods and emotions this is called *emotional contagion*. How many times have you been around someone who is happy for no particular reason and all of a sudden you feel happy?

We have all had the experience of going to work in a foul mood and mope around with a screwed up face hoping that others don't notice. Guess what? They do. You know you do your best work when you're feeling good, happy and there's a spring in your step. As the leader you are the emotional thermostat of your team, if you *are* happy they will follow.

But wait, there's more.

If you want to become a super emotionally intelligent leader then you can switch on what Bloom (2001) coined the "the endorphin effect" in others. This means purposefully doing good intentioned things that make your brain and body release endorphins, which are the feel-good chemicals, into your body.

You can create easy daily rituals for yourself and with your team/family where together you do simple things that have you all genuinely feeling good. For example; have a staff compliment board, weekly themed morning teas such as crazy hat or show and tell afternoons, theme a week that focuses on each of your organisational values, bowling afternoons as part of your professional development team-building...

Dr Pearsall (1998) a psychoneuroimmunologist talks about the importance of developing heart to heart rituals because they connect each person's heart energy, creating coherence. When this takes place, everyone benefits from having their immune systems boosted and a natural cohesion and sense of workplace wellbeing is generated.

LEADERSHIP PRINCIPLE

Other People Will Catch Your Emotions.
Make Sure You Throw Them A Good One!

To sum up this chapter:

- Your brain likes to keep things the same. If you keep thinking the same thoughts and doing the same things, then you are going to get the same results.
- Your brain is designed to keep you thinking in the box. If you want to change your life, your leadership and rid yourself of the disease of the SNL then you are going to have to be prepared to start **thinking out of the box**. Only then, do you truly have the capacity to make new decisions, take new actions and enthusiastically anticipate different results.
- To think differently, you need to learn to run your own brain, master your emotions, and then use these skills to empower others to do the same.

This is the inner world of leadership.

FREE BOOK BONUS

If you would like to keep up to date on the latest news and simple strategies for running your own brain and mastering your emotions we have another gift to offer you. If you go to our website **www.StarsLeadershipInstitute.com** and click on "Resources," then click on "My Brain" you will have instant access to a variety of PDFs you can download immediately.

"They could control my body, but they could not control my mind.

Nelson Mandela

CHAPTER 7

Discover the Future That Lies Hidden In Your Beliefs

Beliefs would have to be one of the most powerful forces within our inner world of leadership. They are more than shapers of our results and determinants of our success.

Here is a little secret we want you to share around. Our beliefs are the key to our future health, well-being and longevity… shhhh more about that later.

In the past, beliefs as a discipline in the area of leadership have been regarded as a soft skill. Generally, beliefs are still the most under-developed area of our leadership capacities. STARS Institute recognises the value and the need for us Mob to develop strong personal beliefs and smart leadership beliefs. This empowers us to define who we are and what we are capable of.

When you think about it, this whole book is dedicated to challenging and changing our non-supportive beliefs. The mother of all disempowering beliefs for First Nations peoples is the SNL *"Blackfullas aren't as good as Whitefellas."*

When we asked for her opinion on beliefs and values, the Hon Linda Burney MP said that *"Core beliefs and values, whether they be those of an individual or an organisation, are intrinsic to how an individual lives their life or the way in which an organisation discharges its responsibilities. As a First Nations woman I know what mine are. Some of them are particular to my heritage, however, many values and beliefs are common across humanity. As an individual, the values of compassion, trust, fairness, strength of conviction and humbleness are important to me. It is important to understand personal values and beliefs can change and grow and are influenced by one's life experiences, the passage of time and the gaining of wisdom."*

It's deadly and affirming to hear Blackfulla leaders articulate what their beliefs and values are. Self-awareness equals greater choice and this alone weakens the secret hold and impact of the SNL. When you know who you are and what core values and beliefs drive you it sends out the message to others that we all have the capacity and right to excel in our fields of expertise and contribution.

Deep down we know we can't sustain ourselves and be good leaders whilst carrying around outdated sets of beliefs and behaviours which contradict our values and no longer serve us or are for the higher good of others.

LEADERSHIP PRINCIPLE

The beliefs we have today will be the reality of the future our kids will have tomorrow.

This chapter is about an "awakening" of our "Self" and our true potential. Do you really get just how much personal power you have to control your life and the direction it is going in?

On the surface you might think, *"Hey, I'm the captain of my own ship!"* but we challenge you to scratch a little deeper. You may find you could be the victim of unexamined beliefs. Perhaps this statement is a little bold. Perhaps it has got you feeling a bit wild. We understand, no one likes to be called a victim.

We do not apologise if our bluntness in this chapter upsets you. It is intended to interrupt your habitual way of thinking about yourself and life. For too long we have suffered unconsciously from the madness of the SNL. This is one such belief that has caused us to become anaesthetised and distracted from reaching our full intellectual potential, spiritual power and enjoyment of life.

As First Nations peoples there are parts of our collective thinking and being that is erratic and shut down. We need to be prepared to look

anew at ourselves, be **willing** to admit we have some crappy beliefs and be ready to **consciously** create empowering beliefs which are supportive and grow us in the direction we want to move towards.

> This is an issue of national importance. How we are wired to think and what we're wired to believe and feel, acts to determine the future our kids will live into.

Are We Screwed Up?

Over the last six years, it has been said to us by other Blackfulla leaders that, *"We are just as screwed up as the people we are trying to help."* Sounds a little disempowering doesn't it? What if we told you that as a people we are not screwed up but we do hold sets of beliefs which are screwing with our physical, emotional, social and spiritual growth and health?

In this new era of colonialism, Blackfullas are still plagued by beliefs which generate constant fear, anxiety and stress. We are wired into cycles of under-achievement, helplessness and dependency, a mindlessness of dysfunction, rolling on from one generation to the next.

> Our current blueprint for leadership is focused on correcting and fixing up what we can't do, rather than strengthening and growing what we can.

Much attention has been invested into trying to solve this vicious cycle at a national level. Whilst this is important, let us also focus on practical, cost effective ways in which we can work on ourselves first and then work with our communities. How can we be expected to be at our best and work compassionately and effectively with others if we too are suffering?

The Secret To Achieving What You Want Is Designing The Beliefs You Need

Think back to Chapter 5, *The Secret of Your Leadership Blueprint,* and the questionnaire you did on your leadership blueprint. Each of those statements was a belief which may or may not be true for you. Together, those beliefs along with other influences have created paradigms that suggest we have limited power to change the direction of our lives and our leadership.

When we begin to distinguish our disempowering beliefs and decolonise our thinking, it is like spring cleaning our subconscious warehouse. This makes room for us to try on new empowering beliefs which shift us towards a fresh paradigm where self-determination starts with us.

Vicki is a master at teaching folks how to turn their visions into victories. Her project management leadership of *Corroboree 2000* is testament to this. Vicki has highlighted four key elements for mastering your inner game of leadership so that you get the outer world results you are committed to.

1. You must **know** exactly what you **want,** you have to have a **vision.**
2. You must **believe** in your **vision** and **believe** in your **ability** to make your vision real.
3. You must **design** or **align** with **beliefs** which are going to drive you **towards** your vision.
4. You must know what beliefs are going to **distract** you from your vision.

We often find that people have great intentions of what they want and organisations have well-thought-out strategic plans. However, when it comes to implementing their intentions and plans it is not uncommon for them to be making decisions and taking action which is in fact moving them away from their vision, rather than towards it.

After a little digging, we find that people are sabotaging their own potential and that of their organisation because their subconscious beliefs are not aligned with their vision.

For example, imagine you apply for a new dream job which has been an aspiration of yours for the last three years. You will be leading a team of 10 people made up of both Blackfullas and Whitefellas. You're very excited and you consciously believe you can do this job with your hands tied behind your back. But sneaking around in the background of your subconscious for the last 27 years is a silent network of beliefs like the ones below which have caused a humming of frustration, jealousy and resentment:

- If you become too successful people will try to pull you down
- Successful people are arrogant and can't be trusted
- It's not culturally appropriate to be seen to be too successful
- You hate it when other people go big-noting themselves
- White people can't be trusted
- Asking people for help is a sign of weakness

The million dollar question to ask here is, Do these beliefs support you and move you towards your vision and aspirations or do they take you away from your vision and aspirations?

REMEMBER!

Your beliefs are stored within your subconscious warehouse.
You don't even know that your subconscious beliefs are running your life.

Announcing....What Is A Belief

Very simply, a belief is a **repetitive** thought that we feel very strongly about and that we hold to be **true**. Beliefs are actually not true or false, right or wrong, good or bad. They are only habitual ways of thinking.

Beliefs can be conscious or subconscious and they are what creates the quality of our life and governs the direction of our leadership.

> ## LEADERSHIP PRINCIPLE
>
> *We will always make decisions and take action in accordance with our most dominant beliefs.*

Discover The Truth About What Our Beliefs Are Designed To Do

Like an internal guidance system, beliefs lead us away from painful experiences and move us towards pleasurable experiences. Remember, your brain gets freaked out by anything that it believes will bring you harm and cause you pain.

At STARS Institute we like to think of our beliefs as huge pairs of funny glasses that we wear throughout life. Mind you, we don't even know we have these glasses on. Every experience we have is filtered through our belief glasses. Everything we listen to or see is given meaning and becomes sorted according to our beliefs of what will move us away from pain and what will bring us pleasure.

Our belief glasses actually determine how we hear and also interrupt what we are listening to.

Has Anyone Ever Said That You Never Listen To Them?

I wonder if we ever really listen to what others are actually saying?

Notice that even as you are reading this book you are interpreting what you are reading according to what the little voice inside your head is saying about what you are reading.

You are automatically having a conversation with yourself about what is written. Much of the information you are reading may be new and your subconscious mind is judging and comparing what you are reading about, with what you already know. It is searching for where it can make connections with existing information so it feels at ease with accepting the new information.

Your brain constantly has to change and rewire itself in accordance with what you are reading and what you are making it mean.

Consider that rather than getting the meaning in the text, you are attaching meanings of your very own.

It's like if your partner comes home and says to you, "I love you" what is it you are actually hearing? You hear the words *I love you* but you make it mean something different, like *they've done something wrong, they want money, something bad has happened*, or *they want sex...*

Human beings are a meaning making machine. As Anais Nin says, "*We don't see the world as it is, we see the world as we are.*"

Revolutionary Results In The New Science of Beliefs

Biologist Dr Bruce Lipton, through his ground-breaking work in the new science of epigenetics, has now proven that your beliefs and thoughts directly control your biology and your behaviour (Lipton 2005).

But here is the mind-blowing part of Dr Lipton's work. Your beliefs also control the healthy functioning of your genes and DNA. It was once believed by the scientific and medical worlds that your genes controlled your biology and were accurate indicators for your future health and well-being. However, the work of Dr Lipton has now shown that every thought we have has a biochemical effect on every cell in our body.

His research shows that genes and DNA do not control our biology but instead, DNA is controlled by energetic messages from our positive and negative thoughts.

LEADERSHIP PRINCIPLE

Your biology is a print-out of your psychology.

Loving Thoughts And Beliefs Help You Grow

Is your life filled with loving, supportive thoughts, beliefs and healthy relationships? Are you generally happy and optimistic, with a singing-in-the-rain attitude? Do you have a purpose to your life and feel affirmed and validated by others? If you do, then hooray because you're consistently nourishing your body with endorphins, oxytocin, dopamine and serotonin which is your body's natural feel-good chemicals.

Dr Lipton (2005 p 115) explains that the quality of beliefs activate a natural growth response in your body which builds up your immune system and stimulates and supports your physiological and psychological growth and development.

Hateful Thoughts and Beliefs Make You Fat, Sick, Old and Dumb

If you are predominately pessimistic, distrustful, angry and negative, have the habit of thinking non-supportive thoughts and hold beliefs that life is all doom and gloom then you are feeding your body with stress hormones such as adrenaline, cortisol and norepinephrine.

Dr Lipton (2005 p 116-24) has named this the *Protection Response*, because it stimulates the body's natural fight-flight-freeze reaction which floods you with the stress hormones. Too much of these stress hormones over time is hazardous because it increases your blood sugar levels, which makes you crave sugar and carbohydrates and store fat, stops the growth and repair functions within your body, disrupts your sleep, impairs your brain's capacity to solve problems and make decisions, breaks down your immune system, speeds up the aging process and kills off your brain cells.

So if you go to bed angry or stressed out most nights, you wake up the next morning old, fat, sick and stupid!

The Truth About Beliefs

By the time we're about six years old we've had enough experiences for our brain and our subconscious mind to draw conclusions about ourselves, other people and the world around us. It is during these early childhood years especially, that inter-generational beliefs get handed down from one generation to the next. This vital period of programming forms the root of our identity, beliefs, rules about life and our emotional set point and patterns of behaviour.

Famous cultural anthropologist, Margaret Mead, discovered in her research that the average child received over 140,000 negative messages about themselves during their first ten years and only an average of 10-20,000 positive messages. Our early programming forms the entire basis of our self-concept and our attitudes towards ourselves, others and the world.

If you grew up in an environment where you felt safe, loved, accepted and understood, chances are that you will have developed supportive self-beliefs. If, however, you experienced separation, rejection and hostility during your early childhood years, then it is probable that you will have developed some self-protective/destructive beliefs.

We either grow up relating to ourselves through the lenses of *being* safe and living in states of growth and expansion OR through the lenses of *being* fearful and living in states of protection and contraction.

The good news is that you can change your life by changing your beliefs (Dr Norman Doidge 2008).

> Simply put.... when you change your beliefs you change your brain, when you change your brain you change your life.

Discover How You Got Your BS

The three ways we developed our beliefs systems (BS) are:

1. Verbal programming. What did you hear when you were young?
2. Modelling significant others. What did you see when you were young?
3. Specific events: What did you experience when you were young?

In this chapter we are only going to talk briefly about how verbal programming creates your beliefs. Modelling the beliefs of other people is very similar to verbal programming.

In Chapter 8, *Find Out How Your BS Shapes Your Life,* we are going to share with you my story about a specific childhood event which had me form the beliefs, *"I'm not good enough"* and *"No one likes me."* You will get to see these beliefs in action and how these two beliefs almost killed me.

Verbal Programming

While you were growing up, what messages did you consistently hear about yourself from the adults around you? What messages did you hear or not hear about the topics of success and leadership?

Did you ever hear things like, *'Don't go big noting yourself; you've got to work twice as hard and twice as long to be as successful as White people; close enough is good enough; never trust the government; you're just as good as a White person; Blackfullas are better at sports than they are at school; that one doesn't speak for me; you can't do that;*

you can never do anything right; you won't win so why try; the rich get richer and the poor get poorer; family's more important than money; you've got to learn to fight and stand up for yourself'...?

All the statements you heard about yourself, your culture and about success and leadership are downloaded directly into your subconscious mind as beliefs. They then become part of the operating programs for your blueprint that is now running your leadership.

Change Is Easy If You Change Your Language

Language is a very powerful means of programming and your subconscious mind is listening to and feeling every word you say. This includes the constant chattering of your self-talk.

Have you ever caught yourself saying something or thinking something your parents or your family used to say to you when you were growing up? Unbeknown to us, as we have grown up we've taken over where the adults left off, enabling our self-talk to contribute to programming our thinking and keeping our beliefs alive.

Just be still for a moment and think of an adult who had a big impact on your life as you were growing up. What messages did they say to you and how did they say them? Notice what you **made** their messages **mean**?

Don't be surprised if you can remember more negative messages than positive messages, remember the brain is a magnet for negativity and is always on the lookout for what is bad, wrong, broken, absent or insufficient.

If we don't know how to interrupt this innate response then we automatically develop a mindset and vocabulary about ourselves and life based on beliefs of deficiency. This is ugly because these beliefs unavoidably generate low trust, low expectations, low self-esteem and low energy for change.

What's even uglier is that this thinking doesn't empower us to be effective problem-solvers. It permits us to be effective problem-generators. If we are focused on what's not working or what is wrong, we get more of what we are focusing on and as a result the problem grows in negativity. Our brains cannot operate effectively when we are coming at something from a place of negativity. It blocks solutions, so we literally box ourselves in and stop solutions from being received.

What is of importance now is that you begin to become aware of how your experiences shape your language, how your language shapes your thoughts, your thoughts shape your beliefs, your beliefs reinforce your language, your language reinforces your thoughts, your thoughts reinforce your experiences...

The average person has around 60,000 thoughts a day and 12,000 internal conversations (Sheehan & Pearse 2012 p 215). The problem is that they are usually the same 60,000 thoughts and 12,000 conversations that they had yesterday and the day before that...

The question then needs to be asked, what kind of thoughts and internal conversations are YOU consistently having with yourself?

Consider that we are subconsciously recycling old language patterns, complaints, beliefs, thoughts and behaviours and passing them on from one generation to the next. As a result, as Einstein said, we are boxed in by the boundary conditions of our thinking.

REMEMBER!

Your beliefs are only habitual ways of thinking.
When you change the way you look at things, the things you look at change! (Wayne Dyer)

How To Get Smart: Stop Telling Yourself You Are Stupid

Have you noticed that we have a habit of dismissing it when someone gives us a personal compliment or positive feedback like acknowledging us for a job well done? It's almost like we resist being told how good we are because it is not a match for the belief and image we have of ourselves in our subconscious warehouse.

What we are good at, is personalising the negative verbal messages we grew up with by turning them into "I" statements?

- I'm stupid, I've never been any good at…
- I don't matter
- I am fat, it's in my genes
- I had a bad childhood
- I wish I wasn't worthless
- I am married to a drunk
- I shoulda, I coulda, I woulda done that
- I'm sick of all the racism
- I was told I was ugly
- I haven't got time for this
- I've got no money
- I'm scared
- I'm a diabetic and I can't eat that, or do that, or have that or…
- I am not good enough
- I am a sinner
- I can't do it
- I am dumb I was never good at school
- I've always picked the wrong man
- I'm a smoker, I come from a family full of smokers
- I've got dyslexia
- I wouldn't be suffering now if she only said sorry
- I'm too strict on my kids or I let my kids walk all over me
- I am a lazy Blackfulla
- I've been bullied all my life

WHOA! Stop there...you get the picture right!

Be mindful of the words you put after "I am" because this label sticks like glue and turns into your life story. Predictably, that is who and what you become. Have you noticed that we will fight harder to defend and reinforce our stories of limitation than we will to accept the graciousness of a compliment!

Listen to yourself the next time someone says something nice about you. Watch how you automatically want to justify the compliment by turning it into a complaint or negative judgement. For example, when people used to say to me, "*Wen, you look like you've lost weight,*" rather than saying, "*Yes I have, thank you,*" I'd automatically be thinking to myself "*Oh is it really that obvious I got so fat?*" So I would respond to them by saying, "*Yeah, I've lost 5kg but I've got another 20 to go and I just don't know if I can sustain it...blah, blah, blah.*"

You see, in my subconscious warehouse I used to have a huge colour poster of me being a super-sized, flabby, fatty boom-ba. I felt awful, hopeless and powerless every time I thought about my body and my health. As a result, I could not consciously hear or accept anything that was in conflict with my subconscious belief that "I am a big fat ugly cow."

Oh, and here is another interesting observation. Listen when two or more people start talking about their past; invariably they end up talking about all the sadness, regrets and gloomy bits. Then a strange phenomenon happens. They will subconsciously get into a weird form of 'one-upmanship' where they actually compete for who has the worst sorry story.

If in doubt try it out. Start a conversation about the SNL or Blackfulla issues in general and watch what happens. Nine times out of ten the conversation will refocus itself from what is possible to complaints of what's not possible. Observe how there is then a struggle to pull yourself out of the story and out of the competitive rhythm.

Due to our brain's attraction to negativity, if this psychology cycle of deflect, reject and complain about "life's good bits" is not recognised, we can become trapped in a state of leadership neurosis. How many times have you managed to talk yourself out of your own greatness and success?

If we're habitually speaking to ourselves in self-deprecating ways we are triggering the release of stress hormones into our bodies, which as we have already learnt impact our cellular and emotional health.

Consider that disempowered belief systems and negative self-talk have contributed to the rise in inter-generational lifestyle disease in Aboriginal and Torres Strait Islander families and communities.

It's Weird But It Works

Cultural safety is a top priority for the STARS Institute and it is within this sacred place that we guide people through highly effective processes to transform beliefs.

Here is one simple process you can do at home today to begin changing your verbal programming and ultimately rewiring your beliefs and writing YOUR leadership blueprint. What is great about this simple process is that it is an easy-to-use tool you can use anywhere any time.

Read through the process a couple of times so you know what to do and it doesn't freak your brain out or you'll come up with a proper deadly excuse for not doing it.

LEADERSHIP PRINCIPLE

You will either have a good result or a good excuse!

Self-Awareness:

You can't change something unless you know it exists.

1. In your leadership blueprint journal, quickly write down everything you heard other people say about you, success and leadership as you were growing up.
2. Highlight all the affirming and supportive messages which we call "I can" messages.
3. Highlight the condemning and non-supportive messages which we call "I can't" messages.

Understanding and Appreciating:

By understanding where your thinking came from you can begin to appreciate that your thoughts are not yours and they are not who you are.

1. Quickly write down all the positive experiences you have had as a leader as a direct result of the "I can" messages.
2. When you have finished writing, squeeze your dominant hand and in a proud and positive tone say YES! Remember this is the YES anchor. Repeat this process until you're naturally smiling and feeling really good within yourself.
3. Quickly write down the experiences you've had which have negatively impacted your experience of leadership as a direct result of these "I can't" messages.

Detachment:

Once you recognise that your thinking is not you, then you have the power to choose to change your thinking if you want to.

1. When you have finished writing the "I can't" messages notice how you are feeling and what you are now saying to yourself. Next, stand up and breathe deeply, animate your face by raising your eyebrows, smile up big, nod your head, shrug your shoulders and in a light hearted tonality say, *"Thanks for sharing! But my thoughts don't define who I am or what I will achieve."*
2. Now picture yourself going into your subconscious warehouse and watch the "I can't" messages going into and out of filing drawers.

Empowerment:

When you get that you have the power to make change you begin to see you have more choices available to you. To expand your options you simply ask yourself new simple questions.

1. Position your chin parallel to the floor, keep your face straight and look down towards the floor while continuing to breathe deeply. When you are in this position you are tapping into your subconscious mind and are emotionally connected to what you are about to ask yourself and the answer you are about to receive.
2. Ask yourself, *"What is a more empowering thought/belief I can have right now?"* Continue to breathe deeply whilst looking down and listen and feel the answer which will come to you.
3. Each time an answer comes up say, *"I got it, thanks"* and give yourself the YES anchor. Notice how you feel.
4. Questions are great because they hook your mind. Whatever question you ask of your mind it has to give you an answer. The quality of your questions will determine the quality of your answers. The quality of your answers will determine the quality of your choices.

The quality of your choices will determine the quality of your decisions. The quality of your decisions will determine the quality of your actions. The quality of your actions will determine the quality of your life. The quality of your life will determine the quality of your leadership. The quality of your leadership determines the quality of your results...

Declaration:

These are simple statements of intention which imply you have embodied and own what you are saying and that action and results will follow. A simple formula to help you exemplify this is: *Be it – think it – speak it – act it – have it!*

1. Now here is the super part. You are going to do what I call, "*The Archie Boy Strategy.*" You are to smile up big, widen your eyes, point to your head and declare out loud and with confidence, "I am a BIG thinker!"
2. You then simply say all the other self-affirming, big, beautiful and bold thoughts you have. Even if you have one new thought, that is awesome. Make sure you anchor it with a huge YES!
3. The final step is to put your right hand on your heart, smile and declare, "*I am the master of my own mind and body, YES!*" Repeat this step until your body feels deadly and confident.

Action:

Inner world possibilities become outer world realities only when you commit to taking consistent action.

1. Hunt out your non-supportive beliefs, thoughts and self-talk. You will be able to distinguish them easily now because they come disguised as the little voice inside your head which delivers the "I can't" messages.

2. Each time you find an "I can't" message, use this process. Once this process is *"in ya bones"* you will notice that the "I can't" messages are replaced with messages of "I can."

REMEMBER!

Have fun with this process.
It's not about getting it right; it's about training yourself to take action in the face of your own resistance!

Crazy – right? Not from a neuroscience perspective and not according to the Universal laws of attraction and expansion.

We invite you to attend one of our programs, where you will be led through a series of powerful experiential processes that will transform your beliefs and rewire your subconscious on a cellular level for ever. You will come to appreciate that the more control you have over your beliefs, your language and your emotions, the more control you have over your life and your leadership.

The education that STARS Institute offers is like finding balance. Remember when you first learnt to ride a bike and your mind and your muscles had to work together to memorise how to learn and master balance. We bet if you haven't ridden a bike in years and you had to get back on one today you could ride it. Once balance is mastered, it is yours for life.

Well our education is like that, only we call it, "getting it in ya bones!" The distinctions you will gain when you participate in our education will be with you for life.

FREE BOOK BONUS

We understand that on your way to mastery you are still going to require support for a while, just like training wheels on a bicycle. We have another gift to offer you. If you go to our book website **www.OutOfTheBoxThinkingIndigenousLeadership.com** and click on "**Free Book Bonuses**," you can subscribe to the Out of the Box Thinking "thoughts of the week." Every week you will receive a profound lesson that will enliven your spirit, touch your heart, empower your life and grow your leadership muscles.

LEADERSHIP PRINCIPLE

Highly effective leaders have support structures which empower their life!

> **To see things differently you
> don't need willpower,
> self-confidence or brain surgery.**
>
> **You just need the courage
> to think the unfamiliar.**
>
> **Your beliefs determine
> your quality of life.**
>
> **Andrew Matthews**

CHAPTER 8

Find Out How Your BS Shapes Your Life

Vicki and I have included my story in the book because we thought it was important that you get to see how easy and automatic it is for us to live trapped inside old outdated paradigms and beliefs which box us in.

This story illustrates how specific events in our life can determine our beliefs and carve out our future. You will get to see how the power of our self-talk and the energy of our emotions play a pivotal role in embodying our beliefs into our brain, body and spirit.

Anatomy of a Specific Event:

a) Something happens in our life (I am sharing my story of the first time I experienced a sense of failure and rejection).

b) We give it meaning.

c) We experience a strong emotion in response to the meaning we give it.

d) We then react in a specific way and take on an identity as a way of surviving what we just experienced and compensating for the failure we feel.

e) The meaning we give the event becomes the "truth."

f) The truth is turned into a belief.

g) Then we are on a lifelong mission to collect evidence to prove the belief is true.

It was a perfect summer's day, the sun was shining and the surf was crystal clear. I was six years old and it was a day I would remember forever. I was with my hero – my Dad.

Dad was teaching me my first lesson in how to fish. He loved his fishing and he was really good at it. He and his older brother Robert had been in a fishing club since they were both young boys. Every second weekend I would watch Dad get all his fishing gear ready and he and Uncle Rob would be off. I could hardly wait until they returned home the next day with a big catch of fresh whiting, bream and flat head. There was nothing better that us Goori kids loved more than a feed of fresh fish.

But this day was just me and Dad and I was the one doing the fishing. Dad covered all the basics of how to fish. He taught me how to bait the hook, hold the rod, cast the rod and keep my balance whilst standing in the surf. Woo hoo! I got a bite and as Dad was helping me reel the fish in, my heart just about jumped out of my chest as he smiled broadly and said, *"Good job, Wendy Ann."* That was the day I fell in love with fishing and I couldn't wait to go again – just me and Dad, fishing buddies.

Two weeks later my world came crashing down around me. Dad was getting ready to go fishing and I ran to him and said, *"Dad I am ready to come fishing with you."* Dad said to me in a matter of fact way, *"Wen, you can't come fishing with me any more."* Man, did hearing those words hurt worse than pulling off a bandaid on a sore that hadn't healed. Ouch!

I was confused and shocked, this wasn't fair, I felt rejected and disappointed. A giant wave of anger swept through my body and I wanted to scream at him, *"No! You can't do this to me, we're fishing buddies!"* I watched him happily packing up the fishing gear and silently seethed inside with anger and resentment. *"How can he be so happy, doesn't he even care that he broke my heart?"* I wanted to run and hide and never speak to him again and yes, punish him for hurting me.

Those simple words changed my life for the next 32 years but they weren't the words of my Dad speaking. They were the words I was speaking to myself about myself as Dad said, *"You can't come fishing with me any more."* You see, in my 6 year old mind, what I heard Dad say was, *"I don't love you any more and you're not good enough to come fishing with me."*

As it turned out, the only person I punished on that day was me.

From that day on, I had a little voice of self-doubt inside my head. It was like a constant companion waiting for every opportunity to judge, criticise or complain about me. I later realised that my whole life was being filtered through this little voice.

So my words became my truth, my truth became my beliefs and my beliefs became my reality. A self-fulfilling prophecy, *"I am not good enough and no one loves me."*

To compensate for not feeling good enough and not feeling loved, I wanted to have everyone like me and tell me how good I was. I became one of those kids who had to be the centre of attention. You know the ones you see in the shops and you silently think, *"Thank God that one's not mine!"*

My life became a tapestry of experiences which proved these beliefs were true.

Dear Mrs Jones You Suck!

I loved playing team sport and I was always in the A Team for all the school competitions. In year 7 I played netball and my coach, Mrs Jones, came to me one Friday afternoon before we were about to go on the netball court and said, *"Wendy, you need to play in the B Team today."* Just like that she said it, with a stern face and no further explanation. I mean, come on lady, I already had my bib on and had warmed up with the girls. I was in the zone.

Ahhhh, I was shocked and embarrassed. *"What will the other girls think of me? I am one of the best players and at the last minute I am being put into the B team!"*

I always had a feeling Mrs Jones didn't like me. In fact, the only time she was ever nice to me was when I was playing sport so having her put me in the B team was beyond disappointment. I was devastated; it was so unfair.

Feelings of rejection, anger and resentment flooded my body. In my world it just proved that Mrs Jones didn't like me and she put me in the B team because she thought I wasn't good enough to play in the A Team.

So I played in the B Team that day and mannnn did I play well! I played my heart out because I didn't want to play in the B Team again. EVER! In the process of an afternoon I went from being a happy kid who loved co-operating as part of a team to someone who was secretly scared of being kicked out of the A Team. I became highly competitive. After all, my survival back in the A-Team depended on it.

Come and See The New Big Fat Black Teacher!

At the age of 21 I graduated as a teacher and this was a huge accomplishment as I was the first person in my family to ever go to university. During my first year I was transferred to a preschool in a little rural town in north Queensland.

My first duty as a new teacher was to interview the parents of the children. I loved meeting the parents and the kids. They all seemed so friendly, I couldn't wait to start. There were only two other Aboriginal families and we smiled up big when we met each other. To be honest, I was so glad to see them that I wanted to hug them like they were *my* family.

What I did find puzzling was that the other new teacher in the next pre-school unit had only mothers come in for their interviews and yet I had both mothers and fathers turn up and some of them even brought in their parents to meet me. During the very last interview on the last day I got to hear why there were so many people showing up. In came this rather loud and happy natured mother. She walked into my office, sat down, smiled and looked me straight in the eye and said, "*Wen, all the other parents have been talking about you and I expected to walk in and see a big, fat, black coon sitting here. But you're here and you are really nice.*"

Now, as you can imagine, a few things flashed through my mind simultaneously like, should I hit her with my left fist, or my right fist?

I was shocked, angry and insulted and for the first time ever I even felt "shamed out" for being a Blackfulla – like there was something wrong with me. The SNL had surfaced again in my life but this was different. I was alone and didn't have my family around me. I was scared. I was wild at that Mum and the community for talking about me and obviously judging me in not-so-flattering ways.

Then I heard the wise voice of my parents and what they had taught me about dealing with racism. "*Wendy, you always have a choice, you can either choose to re-educate people or reinforce their stereotypes.*" Of course, I was going to go with the first option, after all I had just graduated as an educator of children. I didn't think it would have gone down well to be charged with assault and fired on the first day of my first teaching position.

At the same time, my own little voice of self-doubt kicked in and screamed, "*All the parents are talking about you behind your back and she doesn't think you are good enough to be a teacher because you're Aboriginal.*" I just looked at her and smiled politely whilst still wanting to rip her throat out and I said to myself, "*Well lady, I'll show you just how good I am.*" I became driven and determined to prove her and the Whitefella community wrong.

In the space of a 15 minute parent interview I went from being a girl who became a teacher because I loved kids and knew I could make a difference in their lives, into a woman who became a manic high achiever. My classroom was so abundant with fun and magical learnings that even I didn't want to go home when the day was over.

By the end of my first year of teaching, the kids loved me, "that" mother loved me, the parents loved me, the community loved me and I got great first year teaching reports. With the support of Charlotte, the teacher in charge of the other pre-school unit, I even applied for and won an educational coordinator's position in a large regional town.

Although all looked good in Wendy's world, I felt strangely unfulfilled as a teacher.

I Live In A Family Full Of Beauty Queens

Now, I come from a family which is full of beauty queens. Both my brothers, Anthony and Michael, are the most delicious looking Black men you have ever seen. My two sisters, Angela and Nicole, are tall and gorgeous and could be on the cover of any Vogue magazine. In fact, Angela was a catwalk model. When I say beauty queens, I literally mean beauty queens. In 1967, my Mum won Miss Opal and Miss Warana. My sister, Nicole, won the same Miss Opal title in 1991. I entered the same contest in 1985 and did not win because, I later found out, I was not tall enough.

I take after the women on my Dad's side of the family; short, cute and cuddly with big boobs. Not a size 10 in sight.

In 1997 my sister, Nicole, and I were both education advisers with Education Queensland and one morning we were having morning tea with the other women in our office. The women's conversation soon turned into an admiration session about how beautiful Nicole was. Each woman took a turn in eagerly complimenting Nicole while the others nodded their heads in agreement, *"Oh Nicole, you are so beautiful. You have the perfect body, your skin is glowing, you've got lovely long hair, it's just like satin and oh, look at your nails, you're just gorgeous."*

Then in unison, like a swarm of hungry fish, they turned and stared at me and one woman said with a deep seriousness, *"Wendy, what did you get? Oh yeah, you got the brains."* Bursts of thunderous laughter exploded throughout the room.

Nicole and I just looked at each other and laughed along with the women who, by this time, were laughing so hard tears were rolling down their cheeks as they repeated, *"You got the brains, she got the brains."* Although I was used to being compared to Nic, this was a particularly awkward moment I must say. And yes, I was laughing on the outside but trust me, I wasn't laughing on the inside. If I could have run and hidden forever with a life-time supply of KFC and chocolate, I would have.

I was angry at those women for being so rude to both me and Nic. Insinuating that you either have to have beauty OR brains. My little voice of self-doubt began teasing me, *"The girls don't really like you as much as they like Nicole because she's tall, beautiful and skinny – she's the beauty and you're the ugly fat beast. You really aren't good enough are you?"*

The more my little voice of self-doubt teased and criticised me, the angrier I was becoming at those women and sadly and silently the more jealous and resentful I became of Nicole. It was no use me trying to be beautiful – I will settle for having the brains thank you, it was much less painful. Or so I thought. I became known for being very articulate and, some might say, a tad intelligent.

You Don't Have What It Takes!

Since my first year of teaching in that little rural pre-school I had a dream of becoming a successful principal. Within four years I was actively moving in that direction, I had just been accepted into an Executive Development program and was about to go into an acting deputy principal's role as part of my training. I was proud of this achievement and so were my family.

I thought I would do a Masters in Education, specialising in Principal Leadership to develop my expertise even more. During an interview with the then Dean of Education at James Cook University, he said to me, *"Look Wendy, I don't think you have what it takes to complete your Masters, it is a bit above your head."*

I remember thinking, *"That's not fair, how dare you say a thing like that to me you don't even really know me or what I'm capable of."* I felt dumb, rejected, angry and totally let down because I really looked up to this man. I felt sick in the guts and I just wanted to cry. I watched my dream disappearing right before my eyes.

Yet, in that moment, to cover up my upset and disappointment, I pretended to be very professional. Mind you, I couldn't hear a word he said after that, it was drowned out by my voice of self-doubt going off its nut in the most sarcastic tone ever, *"You see, even the Dean of Education doesn't like you and he thinks you're not good enough to do your Masters ya dumb ass. And he knows intelligence when he sees it!"*

Trapped Like a Rat In A Hole

The destructive impact this incident, along with the others, had on my relationship with leadership and who I was as a leader was astounding. By this stage I completely lost my self-confidence and was second-guessing myself constantly. I was trapped in my own mind games. The more I outwardly pretended to be highly professional, the more I inwardly felt like a loser.

Oh, I later went on to became a principal alright but it was only ever in an acting position. Deep down I never believed I was good enough or had what it took to be the principal of my very own school.

Please, Please, Please Like Me!

I was craving acceptance and belonging and I found my life revolved around getting the approval of people. Leadership was such hard work when you've become a *highly competitive, perfectionist, professional, know-it-all* who would rather work alone than within a team.

To the outside world I was the personification of a highly successful, professional Black woman who oozed leadership but my inside world was a mess. I was emotionally exhausted, restless and unhappy and I didn't even know it at the time. I made sure everything looked good on the outside, yet I was barely surviving within. I became so high maintenance I don't know how I stood myself.

I was constantly haunted by the little voice of self-doubt and the silent beliefs that, "*I am not good enough*" and *"people don't like me."*

I became trapped inside an outdated belief system that kept me locked out of living and experiencing a full life.

I let career opportunities slip by because I did not think I was good enough. I felt threatened by women who were in higher positions, made more money, were better looking or smarter than I was. In fact, to be honest, I didn't have many female friends at all. Oh, and of course I didn't trust men but pretended I did.

The only thing I vaguely thought I was good at was being able to talk really well. Most times I felt like a big, fat, fake phony who was always busy doing stuff but never actually experiencing satisfaction, success, fulfilment or happiness.

When Spirit Speaks!

To deal with this inner restlessness, I lived my personal life on the edge; I lived life in the fast lane. I worked hard and partied hard. The motto was, "all care, but no responsibility." The only part of the motto that was true was the *no responsibility* part.

I had a huge vision for the contribution and difference I was committed to making in the schooling and education of Aboriginal and Torres Strait Islander children and their families but I began leading a lifestyle that was perpetuating the very cycles of dysfunction that I was fighting so hard to change.

In 1996 my world came crashing down. My party lifestyle had me hit a brick wall big time and I came face to face with death. I remember my ol' people, my spiritual ancestors, coming to me and saying that I have a choice to live or die and that I could come with them now. And if I was to choose life, then my life would be in the service of humanity and making a REAL difference in the world. I would not take this journey alone but at times it may be lonely. They trusted that I was up to the task and that they would guide me. Each time I demonstrated that I was responsible with the knowledge they gave me, they would show me the next step.

For the first time in a long time I experienced a sense of inner peace and wonder. Something very sacred had just happened; I felt a shift inside my body, inside my mind and from within my spirit.

Was it possible that I could be good enough? Spirit spoke, *"You've been given the gifts of seeing possibility where it doesn't exist, hearing what is not always said and teaching what needs to be taught in order to change the course of people's lives forever."* This, I knew within my heart, was my life's purpose and it was time to step up and be responsible for my life, what I wanted from it and what I wanted to contribute to it.

To Know And Not To Do, Is Not To Know!

Having a long well-established profile and career in education, I knew after hitting the wall that my expiry date was coming to an end. There was something more I was meant to be doing with my life. Hitting the wall was just my ol' people's way of getting my attention because I clearly wasn't listening to the signs they were sending me.

I began thinking in new ways and knew I had to take actions I had never taken before. So as brave as a soldier, and after just having had my first son Lawson, I decided to end my career in education and start my own business as a life coach.

I trained my ying-yang off and yet I was still haunted with the whisperings of, *"You're not good enough and no one likes you."* I did course after course, read every book and I still never felt like I was quite ready to take on this whole new professional coaching career. *Besides, what if my clients didn't like me? What if I couldn't empower them? What if my own Mob thought I was nothing but a big-noter? I'd never get work or referrals or make money. I'd better go and do another training course." Yes, this next course will be the one!*

After much procrastination, the good old gonna, woulda, shoulda, coulda excuses, and lots of self-sabotage, I got sick of swimming around in my own BS (belief system). I finally decided that since I was standing on the edge of the cliff anyway, I might as well jump and learn to fly. And boy, was it scary!

I was completely vulnerable and for a while experienced a sense of having no control. Which for those of you who are like me – a highly skilled perfectionist control freak – you know only too well we would much rather stab ourselves in both eyes with a very sharp pencil than show any signs of vulnerability. Little did I know it at the time but my brain was rewiring itself like crazy and cleaning out the junk of my subconscious warehouse.

I felt the fear and did it anyway and I trusted in the guidance my ol' people gave me. I always saw a little light at the end of the tunnel in all my darkest moments and I began to believe in myself again. For six years I moved forward with my coaching practice and it was exciting and hard work. I battled every day with the little voice inside my head which continued to hum away various versions of, *"You're not good enough stupid; wake up no one wants to pay to work with a loser… bla, bla, bla!"* But I thanked it for sharing and pushed on.

What Do You Mean My BS is Not Real!

The baton of transformation had been passed on to me by my ol' people and I accepted it with an open heart. I knew with every fibre of my being it was my responsibility to use my skills and expertise to contribute to ensuring the social and spiritual success and growth of our Mob…I wanted my work to make a difference and get real results.

In my search for the answers I participated in a program called the Landmark Forum. I thought it was going to be just like all the other professional development training and seminars I'd done. By day two, my life as I knew it was completely turned upside down and inside out. In a good way! I got that this belief about me, "*Not being good enough and no one loves me,*" was not true. It was just a story I made up when I was 6 years old and upset after Dad said, "*Wen you can't come fishing with me any more.*"

I had lived 32 years trapped inside the, 'I'm not good enough and no one loves me' story, a story that I made up. After I realised this, I felt like a heavy burden had been lifted from inside my whole body. I was so freed up and felt genuinely happy and inspired by life but more importantly inspired by myself. It felt completely natural and I remember having this feeling when I was a kid.

I was so happy and liberated that during the next break I phoned Dad to share my breakthrough. I was a buzz of excitement and tears when Dad answered the phone. Poor Dad kept asking me, "*Is everything alright Wen, are you okay?*" Finally, Dad went silent after I reassured him I was okay and I shared my story.

When Dad spoke, I got to hear his story about the day he said I couldn't go fishing with him any more. With love in his voice and in between short sobs he said, "*Wen, you know that I have always loved you! That day I took you fishing with me, that was family day and all the fishermen in the club had their children with them on the beach.*" But in my world, in my 6 year old mind, I never noticed there were other children there. All I remembered was what was most important to me on that day and it was spending time with my Dad.

Dad continued to say that, "*When I went fishing every fortnight it was a time for men's business and it wasn't a place for a little girl, which was why I couldn't take you with me any more.*"

On hearing my Dad's story about those two significant days I realised Dad never ever spoke the words to me, *"I don't love you any more and you're not good enough."* He didn't say those words. I did… it was me! I was the one who condemned me through the words I spoke.

OMG!! I created those beliefs, *"I'm not good enough"* and *"Dad doesn't love me."*

In that moment I experienced a deep respect and love for my Dad that I'd never experienced as an adult woman. All that excess baggage that I had been carrying with me about my past had disappeared.

That day, a huge part of my heart was healed. I wasn't a scared little girl any more who feared rejection and not belonging. I was finally reconnected with my Dad, my Mum and with my own heart… my ol' ancestral spirits smiled down on me.

A sense of personal power stirred within me and I knew I no longer wanted, or had the right, to point my finger at other people and blame them for the decisions I made in my life and how my life was turning out… Dad, Mrs. Jones, the pre-school mum, my colleagues, the Dean of Education…I turned that pointed finger around, right back in my direction and took a good look at myself.

As a result, I learnt two important things:

1. You can't change the past but you have the power to change the meaning you once gave it. It is <u>your</u> story that shapes who you are, so make sure it is a good one.
2. I am 100% responsible for my own life. Therefore I need to be willing to be 100% responsible for the words I speak to myself and the words I speak to other people.

The Birthing of STARS

As I took on becoming fully responsible for my life, my coaching practice was starting to take off and I was delivering leadership programs for small organisations and government departments. My little voice of self-doubt didn't hang around much any more and when it tried to get my attention I simply said to it in a playful voice, "*Thank you for sharing but I am thinking a more empowering thought right now*." Bang! Away it went.

Life has a way of rewarding you when you transform the way you think and what you believe.

In 2007 I met a remarkable woman by the name of Vicki Scott. She was the project director of *Corroboree 2000* and responsible for orchestrating the historical Walk for Reconciliation across the Sydney Harbor Bridge. Like me, Vicki was committed to making a difference in the daily lives of people. Vicki and I were from different worlds, different cultures and different generations and yet we shared the same vision. Vicki and I knew it was our destiny to combine our unique gifts, talents and strengths and create something incredible together. And we have!

We co-founded a not-for-profit company called STARS Making the Difference (now renamed and refocussed as the STARS Institute of Learning and Leadership Ltd). Our vision was to Transform Lives Transform Communities. Within 6 weeks of becoming operational we landed two major contracts spanning over two years and worth over $200,000.

Following one program when case studies were being collected, one of our Brisbane graduates, Christine, shared that when she came into the program she was suffering from severe postnatal depression and her baby was just three months old. Christine was in her early 30's and in a long term relationship.

She had three other children and her eldest son who was 16 was beginning to be violent towards her – she was scared of him. She told us that before she came to do the *Bootcamp 4 Life* program she was going to kill herself and all her children, she had it planned because she didn't want them growing up without a mother. She only saw two choices, either to die or do the program.

We did not know this during the program.

After participating in the program for six weeks she began to accomplish things that never seemed possible to her before. She began to recover from postnatal depression, she got her driver's license, her 16 year old son started being respectful, kind and responsible and was bringing his mates home to talk with her about their problems. Her son and his mates even made up vision boards for themselves on the things that they wanted to achieve. Oh yes, and she was happy and she and her family were alive.

Vicki and I continue to be touched and inspired by the life-altering results people get after completing our programs. It has often been said to us that there are no other programs like ours out there.

I have learnt that there is no place in my life for beliefs which rob me of my power and have me dumb myself down. There is certainly no place in my life to entertain the SNL. I choose to believe that life is awesome and deserves to be lived fully.

It is MY responsibility to leave this world in better shape. It is my vision that my sons, Lawson and Archie, will inherit the gift of self-belief. Our family motto is the next leadership principle and my boys have got this motto in their bones. As a family we start and end the day with our motto.

LEADERSHIP PRINCIPLE

Always Believe in Yourself. Believe in your Dreams.
Believe in others and others will Believe in You!

To this day I still consider myself a high achiever and to be competitive and driven but the difference now is that these are strengths which empower me to contribute and bring joy and transformation to the lives of other people.

What I have learnt from my life so far is this:

1. Most importantly, believe in yourself and believe in your dreams.
2. Know what you want – you will know it when you feel it in every fibre of your being.
3. Surround yourself with people who believe in you and believe in your dreams.
4. Start being the person you really want to be right now – this is not your practice life.
5. Commit yourself to being a life-long learner.
6. Take small actions towards your dreams each day.
7. Never, ever, ever, ever, EVER give up.

> " There is no passion to be found playing small – in settling for a life that is less than the one you are capable of living.

Nelson Mandela quoted this excerpt from Marianne Williamson's poem in his Inauguration Speech

CHAPTER 9

Your Vision Your Victory

Hi again, it is Vicki and I am honoured to be sharing with you my experience and expertise in how to turn your vision into a real life victory.

And right up front, I'll share a little secret with you. When I started as project director for the Council for Aboriginal Reconciliation's *Corroboree 2000* – two days of celebrating the end of the 10-year Reconciliation process which included the Walk for Reconciliation across the Sydney Harbour Bridge – I was scared. While I was delighted that I had been selected to be the person in charge of making *Corroboree 2000* happen, I was also very nervous.

My old beliefs of self-doubt came up, causing me to question whether I could do it. Where would I start? An event of this enormity and profile had never been done before. Fortunately, when I started, I had a supervisor who kept asking me great questions. He caused me to step up and believe in myself because he believed in me.

Whilst I couldn't articulate it at the time, I now know that by getting my fears and self-doubt out of the road, my inner wisdom was allowed to surface. Once I could see and feel the Council's vision for what the two days of celebration would look like, I relied on my inner knowing and experience in communicating with people so I could engage them in bringing THEIR gifts and talents to the table.

I used to say that I did not do anything concrete for *Corroboree* – that I just made sure everyone knew their roles and responsibilities and I set up structures so that issues could be addressed as they arose. Many people, including Ray Martin, said if it hadn't been for me the event would not have happened. Whilst at first my little voice of self-doubt wanted to reject these acknowledgements, I got that my gifts and talents are unique. It was not just about good project management or coordination. I used MY emotional intelligence and spiritual intuition just as much as my mental knowledge.

So how did I manage to successfully work with numerous people, organisations, departments, communities, personalities and positions… to bring it all together?

Firstly, I loved the Council's vision. It was compelling and gutsy given the political climate at the time but more than that, the vision gave a clear message that it is time we start looking for and positively acknowledging what we all have in common and what we all want – rather than only focusing on what is so different about us and using that difference as a division.

LEADERSHIP PRINCIPLE

If you see it, if you believe it, you WILL achieve it!

I was inspired by and believed in the vision. It resonated within me and my values of humanity. I had a very clear picture in my mind about what was wanted, needed and required to have *Corroboree 2000* become a landmark in Australia's modern history. Napoleon Hill (1937) in the famous book, *Think and Grow Rich,* calls this resonance with a vision *"a burning desire"*.

In this chapter we talk about the importance of being clear about what you want and having the burning desire to bring it to life. By now you know that what you focus on WILL become your reality.

Look At What Happens When You Share

As the vision for *Corroboree* was shared around, others started to see how they could contribute by sharing their ideas, resources and talents. Some may remember that on the day of the walk over the bridge, a plane wrote "*Sorry*" in the sky. This was not organised by the Council – to this day, an unknown person was so inspired and committed to the vision of reconciliation that the *Sorry* message in the sky was their gift and contribution to their fellow Australians.

Later, at least one woman who was from the Stolen Generation made it known that the event changed her whole life. She was still suffering the impacts of grief and the trauma of being removed from her family. She decided at the last minute to catch the train up from Wollongong to Sydney for the walk and when she walked onto the bridge and saw the word "Sorry", so much healing happened for her; she said she cried and thought, "Someone cares."

How To Improve Your Chances Of Success Using Two Simple Questions

To begin getting your vision embedded into your bones, first you have to know what it is. The two questions we focus on here are:

1. WHAT do you want?
2. WHY do you want it?

These questions sound like common sense but are often skimmed over, especially the second question, *why do you want it*? Before you can move forward with purpose and precision, it is vital that you are clear about your answers to <u>both</u> these questions.

If you don't get clarity on answering these two questions, the doors of your subconscious warehouse are left wide open and invite unhelpful, unhealthy and un-resourceful thoughts and beliefs to run wild. Such as, "*How do you think you're going to do that?*" "*You've been trying for years to achieve that goal and nothing has worked so far…*"

We are creatures of our bad habits ☺. As you now know, this quality of self-talk is sure to hijack your '*I can*' attitude and redirect your attention to an '*I can't*' way of thinking.

REMEMBER!

Your brain easily gets freaked out if it feels threatened.
I had to constantly learn healthy ways of managing my inner voice of
self-doubt around *Corroboree* if I wanted it to be a success.

How To Engage People Powerfully and Influence Results

When you are clear on these two questions you will discover that you
will be:

- Energised and inspired by what is possible and the difference it can
make in the lives of others. Your brain wakes up and is motivated to
work with you.
- A people magnet. People will be attracted to the vision and want to
be part of it. The vision then becomes a shared vision and has the
capacity to expand in the most amazing ways.
- Able to make decisions with more ease.
- Aware of the power you have to influence the results you want with
the thoughts you think and the consistent action you take.
- A great question-generator. You will start asking questions which seek
out new possibilities and solutions such as, '*What else is possible?*'
- Programming your whole body, mind and spirit for success by acti-
vating your internal success compass.
- Appreciative of your own unique gifts and talents and those of others.

I used the foundation of the framework we are going to share with you
to project manage Corroboree *2000*. It is a 4-step process, partnered with
a powerful set of questions. The framework is applicable to any project,
any person, any life, any age, any event and on any day of the week! It
can be used to launch a new work program or policy, plan a major event,
a birthday celebration, a wedding, a funeral, an overseas trip, the birth of
a child, a party, preparing for a job interview or moving house.

REMEMBER!

We have said throughout the book that our intention is for you to unlock YOUR OWN power and purpose... that is true inner leadership!

There is so much less stress in our lives when we are clear and conscious about what it is we want and why we want it. Have you noticed that habitually we become more focused on what we don't want? And predictably, this is what shows up. There is no real power in thinking this way. You will waste your energy and your life on being consumed by the dramas of trying your best to change everything, and everyone around you, hoping that will move you closer to your vision...

One of my favourite sayings from a Chinese Medicine practitioner is, *"You cannot change anyone else; you can only change yourself and as you do that, you will notice others around you change."*

LEADERSHIP PRINCIPLE

Be the change you want to see in the world.
Mahatma Gandhi

WHERE DO YOU START?

The Secret to Achieving What is Important ...

Plan for Your Success...

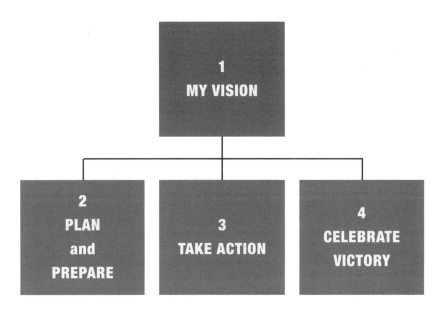

> **FREE BOOK BONUS**
>
> We want to make this chapter really work for you so we have
> another gift for you. It is the work booklet we use in our programs,
> called *'My Vision: My Success Plan.'* If you go to our book website
> **www.OutOfTheBoxThinkingIndigenousLeadership.com** and click
> on "Free Work Booklet," you can IMMEDIATELY download the work
> booklet and begin using it.

You have heard the saying, *"Failing to plan is planning to fail,"*..... Well, it's true! People spend more time planning their weddings, birthday parties and funerals than they do *consciously* planning their life and the direction of their leadership.

Research undertaken by the Harvard Business School on the difference between success and failure showed that only 3% of the people studied were successful, 30% were moderately successful and 67% just existed. The significant difference for the 3% who were successful was that they wrote down specific goals. 30% of the people were moderately successful because they had a general idea of where they were going but didn't have any goals formalised. The remaining 67% were happy to watch the world go by. What is interesting is that people in the 30% category only needed to put in a small amount of effort to jump into the next group (website **www.GetLevelTen.com**).

And consider...... *"To generate fresh ideas we have been told to think outside of the box and then jump back in. Vision building destroys the box and builds a new one. It does not play with the existing paradigms; it changes them."* (*Having Ideas Versus Having a Vision*
      by Roberto Verganti, Harvard Business Review *2010).*

LEADERSHIP PRINCIPLE

Effective leadership requires you to determine if a vision is worth pursuing. If you believe it is, the question is, "Are you willing to fully commit yourself to it?"

Our question for you is how committed to yourself and your vision are you?

STEP 1: WHAT IS YOUR VISION?

Your vision needs to speak to you. It needs to juice you up and have you be passionate about **what** you want and **why** you want it. It is not just words or pictures. It is like putting in the coordinates on your internal GPS – the two core questions will be what take you from where you are, to the place you want to go.

Focus on what makes your heart sing and make sure you 'feel' it in your bones when you are working through the process. If you are passionate about your vision but you feel somewhat hesitant or constrained, you might like to consider whether there is an underlying unsupportive belief that is stopping you from dreaming big and dreaming it into reality. You need to address that first. Chapters 7 and 8 will assist you in this regard.

It's Weird But It Works

You can either use your leadership blueprint journal or the work booklet to answer the following questions.

1. Close your eyes and picture what you **want**? See your vision as if you could reach out and touch it. You'll know it's the right vision because you will feel it in your body and there will be an inner awareness that this is right for you.
2. Quickly empty your mind by writing down any words, statements or draw pictures about what you saw, heard and felt (Page 2 of your work booklet).
3. Either draw a picture/s, mindmap or find a photograph or picture/s in a magazine to represent your vision. Remember the language of the brain is pictures. If you feel good about what you're seeing and experiencing, your brain will commit the vision to your long term memory in your subconscious warehouse. This is Version 1 of creating and crafting your vision. Do not fall into the trap of stressing about having to get it right the first time. Just get started (Page 3 of your work booklet).
4. Look at your vision, smile and nod gently and take 3 deep breaths. As you do, imagine you are breathing this vision into every cell of

your body. Continue this until it feels good and then say, "I rock" and anchor it with a YES! Remember, each of these steps is imprinting your vision into your subconscious warehouse.

5. *Quickly* brainstorm **why** achieving your vision is important to you and important to others. Do it quickly or your conscious mind will kick in and want it to sound a certain way. Let your subconscious mind do the talking and even if it sounds funny or silly, write it down without editing. Once you have run out of things to write read over it, edit it and add to it, then say, "I rock" and anchor it with a YES! (Page 4 of your work booklet).

6. Generate the feeling of strength and pride in who you are and quickly write down what your unique gifts, talents and strengths are that will empower you to succeed in achieving your vision. Then say, "I rock" and anchor it with a YES! (Page 5 of your work booklet).

7. Answer the question, *"How will achieving my vision make a difference in the lives of others?"* Then say, "I rock" and anchor it with a YES! (Page 6 of your work booklet). You are doing well.

8. Write the answer to the question, *"What will my life be like if I decide not to take action?"* Notice how you feel about this but don't allow any low-energy feelings to emotionally hijack you. Then, in big letters, write the words, *I commit to taking action in spite of my feelings.* Underline the words "I" and "action" then say, "I rock" and anchor it with a YES! (Page 7 of your work booklet).

LEADERSHIP PRINCIPLE

Recognise that you always have a choice, so take time to make informed choices.

9. Wendy suggests you stand up and sing the song you created in Chapter 6, *What Everyone Should Know About Running Their Own Brain* – "I'm deadly and I know it." Once you are smiling or laughing,

begin answering the questions, *"What are some of the things that might try and stop me?"* and *"How will I overcome these challenges?"* Again write quickly without editing (Page 8 of your work booklet).

10. What specific beliefs will you need to have which will empower you to accomplish your vision no matter what the challenges? Then say, "I rock" and anchor it with a YES at a level 10 volume. Really feel it oozing into your body! (Page 9 of your work booklet).

11. Go back and look at your vision picture and what you wrote about your vision. Start to speak your vision out loud and anchor it with a YES. Start with *my vision is* or *I want...* Keep doing this until it begins to feel natural and comfortable. Speak your vision with confidence and pride – this is YOUR future. How badly do you want it?

REMEMBER!

You are rewiring your brain and need to interrupt the neural networks which are filled with 'I can't' messages.
Doing things which are totally out of the norm are quick ways to begin breaking old, wired-in, non-supportive habits of thinking.

12. Quickly write down any actions that come to mind that you could begin taking to bring your vision to life (Page 10 of your work booklet). You will turn these actions into goals soon in *STEP 2: What You Need To Do To Plan and Prepare*. But for now, notice how the little voice of self-doubt might be trying to kick in and say, *"How, how, how are you going to do it?"* Remember to *'thank it for sharing'* and refocus your conscious mind. You are almost there.

13. Answer the questions, *"What resources do I currently have which I can use right now?"* and *"Who will help me achieve my vision?"* Wendy suggests you sing the song, *"I'm deadly and I know it,"* and anchor it with a super YES, before you answer the questions! (Page 11 of your work booklet).

STEP 2: WHAT DO YOU NEED TO DO TO PLAN AND PREPARE?

It is time to plan your work and then work your plan. The next important step is to have specific goals. If you don't have written goals, chances are you won't know what you need to do to achieve your vision. Also, you will miss the success indicators when they surround you, such as the right people showing up and doors of opportunity opening up. All this will pass you by.

1, You are now ready to begin your Leadership Plan Overview. Yes! Look back at your vision picture and your actions and choose three actions that you can now turn into goals.

   For example, let's imagine you had a vision to develop a community healing program for five urban communities, targeted at women in the workplace. One of your actions which you suggested in Step 12 was to pull a team of people together to work on the community healing project.

   The **goal** could now be to establish a leadership team of ten people who are from an effective non-government organisation or a key person of influence in each community. It will be their role to contribute their gifts and talents to the development of the program and then account for the delivery in their particular community (Page 12 of your work booklet).

You are probably already familiar with the SMART model for generating goals. It is easy to use so you can "hear" if your goals will move you towards or away from your vision.

It is possible that you might come up with great goals that look and sound awesome <u>but have nothing to do with your vision</u>. People do this all the time.

REMEMBER!

This is good practice at *being* a conscious leader.
It means you are a conscious thinker and doer.

Use these SMART questions, until you feel there is no reason why you cannot achieve your vision and goals....

S = specific and succulent
What do you want to accomplish? Are your goals clear and direct? Are they easy to understand? Do they make your heart sing?

M = measureable and motivating
What quality and quantity of results do you want to produce? Again, make sure you can "feel" them in your bones. Will achieving these measures motivate you to keep going?

A = achievable and action
Are your goals achievable and what actions do you need to take to accomplish them? Can you manage them effectively and have them resourced as required? Do your goals empower you to take more action? Who do you need to engage to help you achieve your goals?

R = realistic and rich
Are your goals a match with your vision? Will they produce the results you want and move you in the direction of accomplishing your vision? Do your goals stretch you and provide rich experiences in your life? Can you feel in your bones that it is possible?

T = time phased and targeted
Are your goals time-phased, so that you are accountable to produce specific results at targeted times to keep you and others on track?

1. Once you have at least three SMART goals you are on your way to creating some actions which inspire you to achieve your goals. Look again at the picture of your vision and anchor it with a YES! Now close your eyes and picture yourself having already achieved the vision and you are celebrating the success. Look back from the future and imagine there are little signposts which are indicators of key actions you and others took that worked towards the overall success of your vision.

2. Open your eyes and quickly write down all the key actions that you saw, heard or felt that were highly successful. Some of the key actions might include;

- Visiting the 5 communities and putting on a lunch for the Elders and key community people to share your vision, invite their input and feedback and ask for a representative to be on the leadership team.
- Fortnightly (or monthly depending on your timeframe) 1 hour *Creation Meetings* with the leadership team to report on the progress of their areas of responsibility, share challenges, offer solutions and celebrate their monthly successes.
- Set up an online forum/Facebook page for the Indigenous women your project is focused on to find out what they want from a healing program, what issues they are dealing with, what they have tried which has worked, and what they have done which has not worked for them and why it hasn't worked.

Once you have finished writing the actions, like Wendy says, you can sing the following words to the tune of the song, "I'm sexy and I know it!" "*I'm going to achieve my vision and I know it*" and anchor it with a huge YES! Remember, you have to do things that are "out of the box" if you want a different result ☺. (Page 13 of your work booklet).

I am curious. Did you notice that your actions may be new or different from what you expected? If they are, great job! It is an indication that you are tapping into the creative energies of your subconscious and are creating inspired actions.

These are not your garden variety actions. Inspired actions make you feel like you are living *in the zone* and you can't wait to get out of bed and go to work…

You are on fire, you feel amazing, you are making all the right decisions and your resilience is high.

3. You are right on track. Now choose a planning format which works best for you. We use this simple one page summary so you can quickly see where you are at. We would suggest that this is a simple way to break bigger action plans into bite-sized workable pieces. We have included this on page 13 of the work booklet.

Vision/ Project Name: _____

Goals	Time Frame	
	Start Date:	Expected Completion Date:
1.		
2.		
3.		

Leadership Team

Name	Position	Expertise/Role

Summary

Action	By When	Who
Goal 1		
Goal 2		
Goal 3		

When you have completed your plan, ask yourself this question, *"What is one action I am committed to taking today which will move me closer to achieving my goals and vision?"*

LEADERSHIP PRINCIPLE

Never leave the site of a new idea without committing to taking immediate action. It creates the momentum of success.

Get loud! Once you have on paper what you want to achieve, what you are going to do to get there, and how you are going to measure your progress along the way, it is time to share your vision with others. Sharing your ideas with others keeps you connected to the WHAT and the WHY. You get more clarity and confidence every time you share.

Yes, it can be scary and challenging. The main concern your mind will be plagued with is a worry for what other people will think about your idea and about you. The fear of this happening to you is so great that it could stop you in your tracks and you will want to go back to life as you have always known it. Back into your comfort box......

REMEMBER!

Your brain has a negativity bias so it is expecting that others will find fault with what you share. So meet the challenge head on.

EVERYONE WHO DOES IT SAYS IT WORKS LIKE MAGIC

Here is what you do to prepare yourself before you share your new ideas and vision. This is such a powerful process which boosts your confidence and gets people to actually engage with what you are saying.

1. Write down every complaint and criticism you think people will have about your vision or plan – or you! Let your mind go crazy for about 5 minutes. Get it out and write it down.

2. Prepare simple responses to each of these criticisms. This process prepares you for any challenges that may come your way and it relaxes your mind so that it knows how to respond in this situation if it comes under threat.

3. Here is what Wendy calls the super-deadly part. One of the first things you do when you meet with people you want to share your vision with, is address the anticipated complaints and criticism right up front.

> For example, you may say, *"If I were you I would be wondering, 'How can you expect me to be on the leadership team for this project when I am already so busy...?'"*
>
> You can then say, *"I see you are doing the job of 2 people at the moment and that can't be easy. So perhaps you can't be on the team right now; I certainly don't want to increase your workload or stress levels. I would value any of your suggestions and welcome your concerns at any time down the track. Any feedback you give us can help this community healing program be a success for our women. Perhaps you can suggest others in your organisation/ community who might be interested in hearing some more about the project idea."*

You need to know that sharing your vision with others is a critical part of the process and the bonus is that when you say it often enough you will find that not only the words begin to flow more easily, but your vision has more clarity for and connection to you. As others see how excited you are about it they will start to believe in you and what you are doing, and even consider ways they can help you bring it to reality.

You need to be aware that some people can be confronted and sometimes so challenged by your new passion to succeed that they may come back with some unhelpful and demoralising comments after you've shared your vision. But that's okay. Remember, you can't change anyone else! You now know how to prepare for that. You can also use the opportunity to go back to your vision and remind yourself why it is important to you, and the impact of you NOT achieving it.

If you continue to get stuck, even after you have tried out the strategies in this book, please contact us via our website www.StarsLeadershipInstitute.com and we will help you out. Our mission in this chapter is to have you achieve your vision.

LEADERSHIP PRINCIPLE

Who you are today actively determines who supports you tomorrow.

When you share your vision or ask for feedback on your plan, remember *the power is in the question*. Consider asking for feedback on your vision based on this approach:

1. The value I see/hear/feel in your Vision is….

2. What I really like about your Action Plan is ………

3. What I specifically like about your Goals is ……

4. What I would like to suggest you think more about is ……

STEP 3: TAKE ACTION

This is where the rubber hits the road. It doesn't matter how inspiring your vision is or how good the plan is, if you don't take action. Without constant action the plan is just words on a page.

A plan without action is like a body without a heart. It needs movement. It needs energy.

LEADERSHIP PRINCIPLE

Knowledge is Power and Action is EMPOWERING!

Here are 6 key questions you need to habitually ask yourself so that you keep your inner world of leadership strong and grounded and you can test and measure your outer world results to make sure you are still moving in the right direction.

1. Am I taking the daily actions I need to stay on track and achieve my vision and goals?
2. Am I achieving my milestones?
3. How am I taking care of myself in body/mind/spirit?
4. What challenges and breakthroughs am I having?
5. Do I need to change any of my actions to achieve my goals?
6. Do I need to look at any of my beliefs to see if they are still serving me?
7. Why is achieving my vision important to me?

FREE BOOK BONUS

Here is another gift for you. If you would like a copy of our 1-page My Vision. *My Leadership Plan workflow* which includes these questions go to our book website **www.OutOfTheBoxThinkingIndigenousLeadership.com** and click on "My Vision. My Leadership Plan workflow" to IMMEDIATELY download a copy.

STEP 4: CELEBRATE YOUR VICTORY

Celebrating your victory is too often forgotten because usually we are so exhausted after it. But celebrations and acknowledgement is equally as important as getting clarity on your vision in the first place!

Everyone needs to feel acknowledged. People want to know that their part mattered and that because of a number of people working together, using THEIR unique gifts and talents, something special was achieved that would not have been possible if they had not come together with a clear intention.

So many of us forget to take the time to acknowledge ourselves and our bodies. We automatically think we have to jump into the next task on our list! No matter how small or grand your success, for your health and well-being to be sustained over time you need to build in down-time.

The 5 key questions in this final step are:

1. How have I acknowledged myself for achieving my vision?
   - First – relax, breathe deeply and regenerate. Take the time to let your body unwind after the vision has been achieved and FEEL what a good job you have just done.
   - Look in the mirror at the end of the day and be happy with the reflection you see looking back at you. Smile up big, take a deep breath and say with love and honour, "Well done, good job, YES!"
   - Do something special for yourself.

2. How am I going to acknowledge everyone who empowered me to achieve the vision?
   - People like to be acknowledged. Acknowledging others both privately and publicly is a much valued habit to build! Be clear about what people have done to contribute to making the vision a reality.
   - It is a time to bring together all parties in some form of ceremony – whether it is sharing a coffee, blowing party whistles or hosting a success party.
   - It is a time to write to individuals acknowledging them for who they are and the contributions they made in bringing the vision to reality. It shows you respect other people and the relationships you share.

3. Identify what worked well, what did not work as well as you would have liked and what could be done differently next time.
   - Identify, acknowledge and <u>learn</u> the lessons. Pay attention to creating safe forums that allow for review and evaluation conversations. It is important you all grow from this great shared wisdom.
4. What am I going to do with the results I produced?
   - Anchor your feeling of success with a huge YES! Create the space for the biggest question of all -- WHAT ELSE IS POSSIBLE?
5. What do I want now?
   - Go back to Step 1 – My Vision

LEADERSHIP PRINCIPLE

Good leaders say I did it...Great leaders say WE did it!

Remember your life is a journey, not a destination. YOU now have the inner capacity to consciously decide the quality of life and leadership you want to have on your journey.

And when you find yourself trapped back in the box of your past, push open the lid and jump out with enthusiasm and ask the world, *"What else is possible for me now?"*

CHAPTER 10

Epilogue

So here it is. The end of the book but only the beginning of you being the leader you were born to be…for yourself….for your family….for your community….and for Country.

Use the resources within this book to begin freeing yourself up from the constraints of the past and the SNL. This is the start we as individuals can take to begin liberating ourselves and, in time, others. Dare to dream a big dream for a future which makes your heart sing out loud and proud… give yourself permission to let yourself out of the box.

Lead the way only you can lead. Share the way only you can share. And remember…. there is nobody like you.

Thank you for the contributions you are making right now to ensure this country is a better place for our kids and our grandchildren and all us Fullas, both Black and White, to enjoy…

Always remember, You Are POWERFUL!
You have all the power you need right now to lead in the transformation you wish for the world.

We would love to stay connected with you, so please LIKE US on Facebook, become our Facebook Friend on **https://www.facebook. com/StarsInstituteofLearningandLeadership** and keep us updated on how you are progressing. We are only a click of the mouse away.

We honour and respect you.

Wendy and Vicki

ABOUT THE AUTHORS

Wendy Watego

Educator, Motivator, Leadership Coach and Author

Wendy Watego is a co-author of "Out of the Box Thinking on Indigenous Leadership" and a co-founder and national program director of STARS Institute of Learning and Leadership, an educational organisation designed to empower people in Shaping Transforming And being Responsible for Self.

Wendy's Mother's Mob are Goenpil, Nughie, Noonuccal people from Minjerribah – North Stradbroke Island –which is part of the Quandamooka Nation in Moreton Bay, off the coast of South East Queensland. Her Dad's family are Aboriginal and proud South Sea Islanders from New Caledonia.

After graduating as a teacher in 1989, Wendy began her professional life as a pre-school educator in Sarina, Northern Queensland. As her career developed she took up a variety of educational leadership positions throughout Queensland, the Northern Territory and Malaysia. This included being the first Aboriginal person to chair the Aboriginal and Torres Strait Islander Standing Committee of the Queensland Teachers Union. She says that this position, along with being the first Black woman to be acting principal of Bwgcolman Community School on Palm Island for six months, has been a big influence driving her dedication to the empowerment and transformation of First Nations communities.

After giving birth to her first son Lawson, Wendy left the education system to establish a coaching practice specialising in healing from inter-generational loss, grief and trauma and transformational leadership. She holds a number of qualifications which include Hypnosis, Neuro Linguistic Programming, Reiki, Life Coaching and PSYCH-K.

After a fortuitous meeting with Vicki Scott at an Indigenous Women's Leadership Conference they realised their common vision of empowering individuals—especially Aborigines and Torres Strait Islanders — and together in 2008 formed STARS. As national program director for STARS, Wendy designs and delivers the STARS programs and they are mind blowing. The programs are dynamic and you literally shift your thinking and your life out of the box of limitations and into the world of what is possible. A curriculum which shifts the way people experience themselves and their lives.

She says that in this role: *"What makes my heart sing and my spirit dance is empowering people to complete their unfinished business and heal from the constraints of the past, to unlock their cultural codes from within their DNA, tap into their true leadership genius and achieve the kinds of results that make a real difference to their lives, the lives of their families and to the lives of their communities."*

Wendy is "blissfully married" to her childhood sweetheart, Ken, and the mother of two young boys, Lawson and Archie. They live on Quandamooka Country in Queensland.

Vicki Scott

Leadership Coach, Business Leader and Author

Vicki Scott is a co-author of "Out of the Box Thinking on Indigenous Leadership" and a co-founder and executive director of the STARS Institute of Learning and Leadership, an educational organisation designed to empower people in Shaping Transforming And being Responsible for Self.

In this role she coordinates coaching programs and delivers elements focused on the principles of project management and mentoring. It's a role for which she seemed destined after a long career orchestrating major national events.

Vicki's early career included being personal assistant to the Governor-General at the age of 18. Subsequently she became executive officer for Lowitja O'Donoghue at the time she was Chair of the Aboriginal and Torres Strait Islander Commission (ATSIC).

When Lowitja retired, Vicki moved to the Department of the Prime Minister and Cabinet and became the project director for *Corroboree 2000*. She played a pivotal role in organising the events including the occasion when all of the nation's political and indigenous leaders were on stage together at the Opera House and the following day's Walk for Reconciliation over Sydney Harbour Bridge. More than 250,000 people crossed the bridge during the seven hours it was closed.

After that, Vicki and her husband decided to return to Queensland and she took on the task for the Queensland Premier's Department of coordinating the 2001 Commonwealth Heads of Government Meeting (CHOGM) which would include more than 700 motorcades. September 11 then caused it to be delayed for six months and be held at Coolum.

Based on the experiences organising CHOGM, Vicki went on to develop a Best Practice Framework for Major Events which is still the model for all state emergencies as well as a marketing tool to attract major events.

A series of personal and family illnesses led Vicki to re-evaluate what she wanted to do with her life. After a fortuitous meeting with Wendy Watego at an Indigenous Women's Conference they realised their common vision of empowering individuals—especially from the indigenous population—and together in 2008 formed STARS.

Vicki was born and grew up in Barcaldine, Queensland, one of seven children. After years of moving around the country with her husband, Richard, while he served in the Navy, they now live on the Sunshine Coast of Queensland. They have been married 39 years and have two married adult children and one grandchild.

RECOMMENDED
RESOURCES

SELF-EMPOWERMENT CHECKLIST

Below is a checklist you might like to consider to keep yourself moving in the direction of your vision – or when self-doubt comes up and things just don't seem to be going the way you had expected.

- ✓ Use your leadership blueprint journal/file.
- ✓ Are you clear on what you really want in your life and what you are committed to?
- ✓ Does what you want make you want to smile? Does it make you feel good?
- ✓ Who do you need to be to accomplish the things in life which matter to you?
- ✓ What actions are you consistently taking to move you in the direction of what you want or are committed to?
- ✓ Are your thoughts, feelings and behaviours, matching what you want?
- ✓ When you are experiencing being stuck in an area of your life which matters to you…...ask yourself what impact this is having on you and other people in your life… AND what pay-off do you get out of choosing to stay stuck?... Notice if this is an habitual pattern of yours and whether it is serving you For the Highest Good of All.
- ✓ Practice saying YES to the things you do want and NO to the things you don't want.
- ✓ Notice what activates you experiencing being empowered and what activates you experiencing being disempowered.
- ✓ Practice acknowledging yourself and others daily.
- ✓ Read at least one page of an inspiring book or piece of text each day.
- ✓ Practice Random Acts of Kindness.

✓ Practice Feeling what it would be like to have already accomplished all the things that matter to you and then take some massive action.

✓ Be grateful each day for what you have – "an attitude of gratitude."

✓ Take consistent action on the things you are committed to achieving even when you don't want to.

✓ Smile, breathe deeply, meditate/visualise, and speak with love and kindness.

✓ Go for a walk in nature, drink lots of water.

✓ Hang out with happy, positive, motivating people.

REFERENCES

BOOKS

Behrendt, Larissa (2012) *Indigenous Australia for Dummies.* Queensland, Australia. Wiley Publishing Australia Pty Ltd.

Bloom, William (2001) *The Endorphin Effect: A Breakthrough Strategy for Holistic Health and Spiritual Wellbeing.* Great Britain. Piatkus Books.

Burrell, Tom (2010) *Brainwashed: Challenging the Myth of Black Inferiority.* USA. Smiley Books.

Covey, Stephen R. (1990) *Principle Centred Leadership.* New York USA. Summit Books.

Covey, Stephen R. (1989) *The 7 Habits of Highly Effective People: Powerful Lessons in Personal Change.* Free Press, a division of Simon and Schuster Inc.

Cunneen, Chris (2001) *Conflict, Politics and Crime Aboriginal Communities and the Police.* New South Wales, Australia. Allen & Unwin.

Doidge, MD, Norman (2008) *The Brain That Changes Itself.* Victoria, Australia. Scribe Publications.

Edwards, Coral and Read, Peter. (1989) *The Lost Children.* Australia. Doubleday, a Division of Transworld Publishers Pty Ltd.

Emoto, Masaru (2003) *The True Power of Water: Healing and Discovering Ourselves.* New York, USA. Atria Books.

Episkenew, Jo-Ann (2009) *Taking Back Our Spirits: Indigenous literature, public policy, and healing.* University of Manitoba Press.

Goleman, Daniel (1996) *Emotional Intelligence: Why It Can Matter More Than IQ.* Great Britain. Bloomsbury.

Goleman, Daniel (2002) *The New Leaders: Transforming the Art of Leadership into the Science of Results.* Great Britain. Little Brown.

Gooda, Mick (2012) *Social Justice Report 2012*. New South Wales, Australia. Australian Human Rights Commission.

Hawkins, David (1995) *Power VS Force: The Hidden Determinants of Human Behavior*. USA. Hay House.

Hay, Louise (1984) *You Can Heal Your Life*. Hay House Inc.

Heer, Dr Dain (2011) *Being You, Changing the World: Is Now the Time?* Big Country Publishing USA.

Hill, Napoleon (1937) *Think and Grow Rich*. Wilshire Book Company. USA

Lippmann, Lorna (1981) *Third Edition Generations of Resistance Mabo and Justice*. Melbourne, Australia. Longman Cheshire Pty Ltd.

Lipton, Bruce (2008) *The Biology of Belief: Unleashing the Power of Consciousness, Matter & Miracles*. USA. Hay House Inc.

McGrath, Ann (1995) *Contested Ground Australian Aborigines Under the British Crown*. New South Wales, Australia. Allen & Unwin Pty Ltd.

Matthews, Andrew (1999) *Happiness in a Nutshell*. Queensland, Australia. Seashell Publishers Pty Ltd.

Miller, James (1985) *Koori A Will To Win. The Heroic Resistance, Survival & Triumph of Black Australia*. Australia. Angus & Robertson Publishing.

Moreton-Robinson, Aileen (2007*) Sovereign Subjects: Indigenous Sovereignty Matters*. New South Wales, Australia. Allen & Unwin.

Pattel-Gray, Anne (1998) *The Great White Flood: Racism in Australia*. USA. Oxford University Press.

Pearsall, Paul (1999) *The Heart's Code: Tapping the Wisdom and Power of Our Heart Energy*. New York, USA. Broadway Books.

Pert, Candace (2003) *Molecules of Emotion: the Science Behind Mind-Body Medicine*. New York, USA. Scribner.

Peterson, Nicolas and Sanders, Will (1998) *Citizenship and Indigenous Australians: Changing Conceptions and Possibilities*. United Kingdom. Cambridge University Press.

Ramsland, John and Mooney, Christopher (2012) *Remembering Aboriginal Heroes*. Victoria, Australia. Brolgas Publishing Pty Ltd.

Reynolds, Henry (2013) *Forgotten Wars*. New South Wales Publishing. University of New South Wales Press Ltd.

Sheehan, Martina and Pearse, Susan (2012) *Wired for Life Retrain Your Brain and Thrive*. Australia. McPherson's Printing Group.

Sheehan, Norman (2012) *Stolen Generations Education: Aboriginal Cultural Strengths and Social and Emotional Well Being*. Linkup (Qld) Aboriginal Corporation and Swinburne University of Technology.

Sykes, Roberta (1986) *Incentive Achievement and Community: An Analysis of Black Viewpoints on Issues Relating to Black Australian Education*. Sydney Australia. Sydney University Press.

The Aboriginal Tent Embassy: Sovereignty, Black Power, Land Rights and the State. Oxon. Routledge, Edited by Foley, Gary and Schaap, Andrew and Howell, Edwina (2014)

Tolle, Eckhart (2000) *The Power of Now: A Guide to Spiritual Enlightenment*. Hodder Headline Australia.

Tolle, Eckhart (2005) *A New Earth: Awakening to Your Life's Purpose*. Penguin.

United Nations Declaration on the Rights Of Indigenous Peoples. Australian Human Rights Commission.

Zolli, Andrew and Healy, Ann Marie. (2012) *Resilience: Why Things Bounce Back*. London. Headline Publishing Group.

REPORTS AND PAPERS

Australian Reconciliation Barometer 2012: Comparing the attitudes of Indigenous People and Australians Overall. Research by Auspoll Pty Ltd for Reconciliation Australia.

Bringing Them Home: Report of the National Inquiry into the Separation of Aboriginal and Torres Strait Islander Children from Their Families. April 1997.

Burgmann, Verity (2003) *Power, Profit and Protest: Australian social movements and globalisation.* Allen & Unwin

Closing the Gap: Prime Minister's Report 2014. Australian Government.

Dr Irene Watson (25th May 2012) *Legal System Criminalises Aborigines, says lawyer.* Des Ryan of InDaily. Crikey Independent Media. Independent Minds.

Kerwin, Dr Dale (August 2007). *Aboriginal Heroes: Dundalli a 'Turrwan', an Aboriginal Leader 1842-1854.* Griffith Institute for Educational Research.

Lowe, David (1994) *Forgotten Rebels: Black Australians Who Fought Back.* Manuscript. Sydney, Australia.

National Anti-Racism Strategy 2012 Australian Human Rights Commission.

Tatz, Colin (1999) *Discussion Paper: Genocide in Australia.* Canberra Australia. Australian Institute of Aboriginal and Torres Strait Islander Studies.

TELESEMINARS

Buczynski, Ruth (2013) A webinar Series with Dr Ruth Buczynski. National Institute for the Clinical Application of Behavioural Medicine. USA.

Hanson, Rick (2013) *Transforming The Brain through Good Experiences.* A webinar Session with Dr Ruth Buczynski. National Institute for the Clinical Application of Behavioural Medicine. USA.

Siegel, Dan, MD (2013) *The Mind Lives in Two Places: Inside Your Body, Embedded in the World.* A webinar Session with Dr Ruth Buczynski. National Institute for the Clinical Application of Behavioural Medicine. USA.

VIDEOS

Krawitz, Tony and Dale, Darren and Hooper, Chloe (2011) *The Tall Man: Life In Paradise, Death In Custody* Based on book by Chloe Hooper.

Perkins, Rachael and Dale, Darren (2008) *First Australians*. Produced by Blackfella Films

Pilger, John (1985) *The Secret Country: The First Australians Fight Back*. Produced by Alan Lowrey, Central Independent Television.

Tarantino, Quentin (2013) *Django Unchained*. Movie by Columbia Pictures & The Western Company, written and directed by Quentin Tarantino.

WEBSITES

Civil War Trust. *Slavery in the United States*. Website *www.civilwar. org/education/history/civil-war-overview/slavery.html*

Creative Spirits. Website www.creativespirits.info *Racism in Aboriginal Australia*.

History. *Slavery In America*. Website *www.history.com/topics/black-history/slavery* and www.slaveryinamerica.org

Levelten Interactive. *The Importance of Goals*. Website www.get-levelten.com